My Apprenticeships

Colette ❧❧ MY APPRENTICESHIPS

Translated by Helen Beauclerk

FARRAR STRAUS GIROUX
New York

Copyright 1957 by Martin Secker & Warburg, Ltd.
All rights reserved
First published in the United States of America
by Farrar, Straus and Giroux, Inc., 1978
Translated from the French, *Mes Apprentissages*
Printed in the United States of America

My Apprenticeships

I HAVE never had much to do, in the course of my life, with men of the sort that other men call great. They have not sought me out. For my part, I have shunned them, saddened to find them, for all their renown, already on the wane, already anxious to fit their niches, to live up to their reputations, a little strained, a little broken down, secretly begging for mercy and determined to "put over" charm by exploiting their weaknesses, when not attempting to dazzle by a forced display of their declining light.

If they do not appear in these "Recollections" it is that I have been guilty of preferring—whether male or female is of no consequence—obscure beings, rich with a savour that they withheld, that they refused to yield to commonplace appeals. Some, who have roused my curiosity almost to the point of passion, were merely hesitant, uncertain of how best to disseminate their most precious essence. They behaved like the greedy who affect to despise *homard à l'américaine* because they are not sure of picking it out of its shell with the required dexterity. But maybe I had the true, the lustral gesture—with a handful of water your Italian guide, as he goes by, reawakens the sleeping gold of underground mosaics. A tear, a splash perhaps, and my favourites relented.

I glory in nothing else than in having crossed the path of these obscure, richly-flavoured folk. Sometimes their names, useless encumbrances, have faded from my mind, but if I grapple with them they once more become inscribed beneath the appropriate features, which are slow to fade. The most deeply engraved are not of people who have played decisive parts in my life. I have it in me to keep a cherished corner for the chance acquaintance as well as for the husband or relation, for the unexpected as fondly as for the everyday. That is why, for instance, I have been able to give without love, quite impersonally, a place of honour to the young man whom I watched pretending to get drunk and smoke opium. It is very much less difficult, in any case, to drink and smoke than to make a show of it, and abstinence, a rare thing in any walk of life, reveals a bent for defiance and virtuosity. What then was my young ascetic after, tacking to and fro between drinking-bout and opium-den, yet always sober? He could not help telling me—I who neither doped nor tippled. All he wanted was to feel himself surrounded, supported and warmly enclosed by genuine drinkers and fervent addicts. He was at a loss to put it into words, it came out in scraps of conversation, and I understood everything one day when, instead of speaking of their "drunkenness", he let slip the words "their trust".

So far as wine was concerned he managed easily enough, deftly mixing soda water and champagne. Opium gave him more trouble and sometimes made him feel sick. But a need's a need! What he needed was the fleeting intimacy, the confessions, the disarmed young bodies strewn about him, and the sorrowful felicity of resting his forehead on a shoulder, a breast that did not turn away, of being united in a half-sleep with inaccessible companions.

I also knew a little girl of eight years old who let her mother call her for a long while, far away in the park.

Closely hidden, she listened to the voice that drew near, that receded, wandered, changed its tone, became strange and hoarse by the well and by the pond. She was a very gentle little girl, yet she already knew too much, as you can see, of the various terrible ways of giving oneself pleasure. She would come out of her hiding-place at last and run wildly forward, flinging herself into her mother's arms, panting as though out of breath: "I was at the farm—I—I was at the bottom of the kitchen garden—with Anna—I—I——"

"What will you do worse," I asked her once, reproachfully, "when you are twenty?"

She half closed her delicious blue eyes, stared away into the distance. "Oh, I'll find something," she said.

But I fancy she was boasting. I was surprised to see her play her game twice in front of me. She asked for no promise, no complicity on my part, she seemed to be quite sure of me, as other sinners were in later years, overcome by the bliss of confession and the need to mature under the eye of a human being.

I knew an excellent creature, one of those women who, by nature and power of reasoning, are the lush meadows, the over-flowing granaries of men. She was the friendly mistress of a friend of mine whom I shall call A. With her he found relaxation, affectionate as well as amorous attentions, sound cooking, orangeade of an evening, aspirins in thundery weather, and a sensuality unfailingly benign. He would leave the good Zaza, go away and forget her, come back and find her in front of her log fire between her toy terrier and some unknown man for whom she was also, no doubt, dispensing herb tea and a cordial night. Was B., A.'s friend, a trifle jealous of this restful relationship?

"Be careful," he said to A.

"What are you talking about?"

"That woman. Most dangerous. A bloodsucker. Her unearthly pallor, the infernal red of her hair. . . ."

"Don't be funny. It's dyed."

"Dyed or not, old man, you've no notion of the terrifying change that has come over you lately. I can see it in your temper, in your work. Even your health! That kind of lightning decline is *always* caused by a *femme fatale*. Zaza is clearly a *femme fatale*. You are heading straight for disaster."

A. laughed at his friend and continued to visit Zaza, to forget her, to return to her as chance dictated, to take her out to good, heavy, well-chosen dinners in the Halles quarter. One evening he invited B. to share their meal. After the dessert he got up and, in all innocence, left them.

"Goodbye, my dears. I've a committee meeting at ten o'clock. Drink my health in your brandy. You'll see Zaza home, won't you, old chap, if she's had a spot too much?"

Alone with Zaza, B. soon made her aware of the deep suspicion, the terrified concern that she inspired in him. "A woman like you . . . born to torture and to ruin. Oh! you can't fool me! That idiot A.! Charming of course, but no brains to speak of. He couldn't understand. . . . What do you say? Oh! Nonsense! I am still able, thank God, to see through . . ." And so on.

About midnight B. was bowed in tears over Zaza's white hands. She gazed down, pursing the corners of her large, benevolent mouth. She did not say a word to our friend A., but began from that moment to assume, for B.'s benefit, the full-dress character of the old-fashioned *femme fatale*. She called him to her, forbade him the house, called him back, carved the four letters of her name on the wretched man's wrist with a piece of broken glass, gave him appointments in taxis, crowned her scarlet hair with sprays of jet, wore black lace underclothes and, most outrageously of all, refused to give herself. So much so that B., to his own amazement, was compelled to believe in the ghoul he had invented, and A. became anxious about his friend.

"What is it, old man? Your liver? Your bladder? See a doctor, take a cure, do *something*. You can't go on like this. You look to me as if you were going to pieces."

He did not know how near the truth he was, for B., eating too little, sleeping badly, catching cold at the slightest provocation, was smitten suddenly, like a man bewitched, by a distemper that carried him off almost unawares. Photographs of Zaza found under his pillow, among his private papers and scattered through his business files, went a long way towards healing the grief of the widowed Madame B.

Zaza herself, as she sat knitting herself a little sky-blue pullover, told me the story as I have sketched it here. We were alone, and she took her time, elaborating her tale with frequent: "and the best of it was . . . So there was poor old B. growing absolutely frantic. It isn't that I care much personally for black lace, but there's something about it . . .", and through it all she kept the same roguish air, her pleasant, mature face mischievously puckered, as though she were telling me a good, though slightly exaggerated joke. She ended with a gesture of unconcern that would have sent shivers down a more sensitive listener's back, and the sententious observation: "One should not tempt the Devil, even out of stupidity. B. was an ass: he tempted the Devil."

I can only be thankful, today, that I absorbed nothing from my shadowy friends, learned no effective lessons either in dazzling virtue or resplendent vice, remained immune to influences insidiously diffused and even to direct infection. Occasionally, in my extreme youth, I found myself sighing to "be somebody". If I had had the courage to express my wish fully, I should have said "somebody else". But I soon gave it up. I have never succeeded in becoming somebody else. Dear patterns of a passionate excellence! Dear evil counsellors! Was it all I could do, to love you with a love and a horror that were equally disinterested? Forceful personalities have passed before me, paraded and given of their light. Not in vain, since they remain luminous and pleasing. But I discouraged them. Not to copy is always to discourage. An attention that goes only to feed curiosity looks like impertinence. And I have copied neither the good nor the others. I have listened to them, watched them, which is the perfect way of inspiring the good with an angelic melancholy and provoking the contempt of the reprobate —I use the word in its theological sense. The voice of the reprobate is warm and full of assurance; it never hesitates. So it was, for example, with the voice—major in tone, true in pitch—of Madame Caroline Otero, who imparted to me, years ago, to no purpose and without undue insistence, many great truths.

I knew her very slightly. It may seem surprising to find her name at the very beginning of my recollections. It comes to me aptly to give these pages their right colour. Twenty pages on the ephemeral—vivid, bracing, mysterious; twenty lines on the eminent and the venerable that others have praised and will praise; a sense of wonder at the commonplace, a tendency, every now and then, to yawn with boredom at the noisy "Ahs!" and "Ohs!" that the world exclaims in face of a prodigy, a Messiah or a cataclysm—that is, I think, my rhythm.

As it happens, I remember Madame Otero with pleasure. I might have been able to garner, perhaps, from lips more august than hers, words of wisdom rich in echoes that would have led to my greater profit and enlightenment! But august lips are not so prodigal. I have asked for compensations from the unknown and the come-by-chance, and they have sometimes given them to me, rather in the way the coconut tree bestows its nuts—plump on the head! Madame Otero, upright in the middle of that period in my life when I was exploring the possibilities of earning my own living, had not the faintest resemblance to a coconut tree. She was purely ornamental. Like all luxuries, she was curiously and variously instructive, and merely to hear her made me rejoice that the early stages in one of my careers should have set her in my way.

"You look a bit green, my girl," she once said to me. "Don't forget that there is always a moment in a man's life, even if he's a miser, when he opens his hand *wide*...."

"The moment of passion?"

"No. The moment when you twist his wrist."

She added: "Like this," and made a screwing movement with her two clenched hands. You seemed to see the blood flow, the juice of fruits, the gold, and goodness knows what else: to hear the bones crack. Can you picture me twisting the miser's wrist? I laughed, I admired; there was nothing else for me to do. Magnificent creature! She was, at the time of our first meeting, reaching the age when the women of today consider it necessary to practise sad, gymnastic, restrictive measures in order to disguise and preserve their precious forty-fifth year. Madame Otero did not dream of any self-denying ordinances. I may have learnt nothing from her rare remarks—she was not a great talker, at least not in French—but I had the good luck of being with her behind the scenes, away from the public ceremonies, the suppers and dress-rehearsals of the music hall stage that held her rigid in her gala corsets, her huge breast plate of jewels plastered to her chest. A motionless icon—alive as a tree laden with hoar-frost is alive, only in its glittering. I infinitely preferred another Lina, no less full of condescension, who used to call out to me, familiarly: "Coming to eat my *puchero* on Zaturday? Come early and I'll play you a game of bezique before dinner."

I answered her with the same vague familiarity, and from the moment I set foot upon her doorstep I was happy. A child seldom finds enchantment in the actual palace it has imagined for itself beforehand. Madame Otero's house never disappointed me. Its owner was like a caryatid, carved in the fashion of the period when I was still vacillating. You cannot be intimate with a caryatid, you can only gaze at it. In Madame Otero I gaze upon the landscape of my thirtieth year, or thereabouts. The setting of her private life lingers in my mind, a memory something better than clear-cut—a softly shaded, precise, essential impression of certain fine old pieces of furniture anchored in a sea of satin, which was perhaps embroidered with Japanese storks, and probably foaming with so-called *appliqué* lace. If it was not Otero's room that was given over to a flamboyant Louis Quinze, then it was some other "dainty nest" in the Rue d'Offémont, or the Rue de Prony, or the Avenue de Villiers. What has become of that serene, delicate blue, stretched on the walls, falling from the testers of beds, draped in festoons about windows and glass doors? And that strawberry pink, those dawn-coloured brocades, and the rich damasks that "stood up", as the saying is, by themselves?

The homes of the Lianes, the Linas, the Mauds, the

Vovonnes and the Susies (these pet-names are fictitious) were all of a "crushing" splendour. They had to be, since it was always a question of somebody crushing somebody else. Two salons were better than one, three better than two, even though grandeur had to be sacrificed to quantity. The stifling style was still far from its decay, and you were suffocated with furniture. At a house-warming party you simmered in the steam. It must be remembered that I am speaking of a time when luxury treated domestic hygiene and sport as the least of its handmaidens. Many an "Arab boudoir" had no window. Designers of automobiles worked in humble collaboration with the great milliners, and limousines were accommodated to the size of hats. I can still see Madame Otero's blue Mercedes, a hat-box for aigrettes and ostrich feathers, which was so narrow and so high that, when it rounded a corner, it drooped and sank gently on its side.

Even the stage had a rough time with fashion in those days when the long corset pushed up women's breasts, lowered their buttocks, hollowed their bellies. Germaine Gallois, an inflexible and embattled beauty, refused to act any "sitting" part. Sheathed in stays that started under the armpits and finished near the knees, fitted with two iron springs down the back, two others down the thighs and a *"tirette"* (I am giving you the current term) firmly strapped between her legs to keep the structure in place —an operation that moreover required a staylace six metres long—Germaine Gallois remained on her feet from eight-thirty till midnight, *entr'actes* included.

It is only fair to say that the bijou-residences relaxed once the house-warming was over, and grew mellower with time and use. Little yapping dogs made their appearance, together with a pet monkey, the New Year gifts of porcelain vases, the palms and aspidistras, the portraits by Ferdinand Humbert, Prinet, Roybet, Antonio de la Gandara. Cushions for chaises-longues and day-beds, Spanish shawls draped across the shoulders of baby-grands, statuettes, mantelpiece ornaments, boxes of candied fruits or chocolates, Chinese knick-knacks and lion skins. Occasionally some violent personal taste would burst irrepressibly through, exploding like dynamite. This was not the case at Madame Otero's, but to make everything perfect in my eyes it was enough that my hostess should be enjoying her late afternoon in silk stockings and well-worn mules, a chemise and a petticoat underneath her teagown, which she took off as often as not and replaced with a bathwrap. The hundred and ninety-two cards and the rosewood marker in front of her, an ashtray at her right hand, a glass of anisette at her left, and she was a queen.

Silence and deep absorption in the game took all expression from her face. It did admirably without. For many long years it seemed to scorn to grow old. Madame Otero, who presumably boasted Hellenic blood, had the muscular neck, the stubborn profile of the classic Greek statue; there was nothing in her hands and feet of fluttering, Spanish delicacy. Between her bunches of thickly-growing hair, her little sheep's forehead remained smooth and pure. As Reutlinger's photographs will tell you a hundred times over, "Lina's" nose and mouth were ideals of simple modelling and oriental calm. I am not afraid to say that, from her rounded eyelids to her greedy chin, from the point of her velvety nose to her famous, softly curved cheeks, Madame Otero was a masterpiece of convexity.

"Zit down," she would say. "Cut. Maria, give her a glass of anizette." Her companion, Maria Mendoza, a decayed Spanish gentlewoman of good family who looked like a bony English bay mare, obeyed with great and slightly terrified haste, and the game of bezique, stern enemy of conversation, began. From beneath eyelids that Time had scarcely bruised, Lina watched my hands.

"Two hundred and fifty to zay . . . Two hundred and fifty to zay . . . Two hundred and fifty zaid . . . Fifteen hundred . . ."

She was perfectly well able to pronounce her "s's" correctly, but she kept this small effort of articulation for the stage and her more select acquaintance.

The excitement of the game increased; the bathwrap was allowed to fall carelessly open, the chemise to slip down. Deep in the shadowy hollow between her breasts —which were of a curious shape, reminding one of elongated, lemons, firm and upturned at the tips—a jewel drooped, hooked on apparently at random, sometimes real, sometimes false, seven rows of glowing, pinkish pearls, or a string of stage glass beads, or a heavy diamond. Only the smell of the *puchero* and an imperious appetite could tear Lina from bezique. Standing up, tall and supply erect, her waist still slim above a rump that was her especial pride, she would yawn loudly, thump her exacting stomach with her fist and, followed by her guests, would go downstairs, singing in a true-pitched, metallic voice:

> *"Tengo dos lunares*
> *Tengo dos lunares*
> *Una junta la bocca*
> *El otro donde tu sabe . . ."*

No men were invited and no rivals. The official lover was bandaging his damaged wrist elsewhere. We took our places beside Lina, one or two ageing friends and I, who was not old but colourless.

A true feast for the hearty eater is never the regular dinner of *hors d'œuvres*, followed by *entrée* and roast. On that point Madame Otero and I were entirely agreed. A *puchero*, with its beef, its knuckle of ham and fat gammon, its boiled fowl, its *longazizas*, its *chorizos*, all the vegetables of the *pot-au-feu*, its mountains of *garbanzos* and sweet corn, that is the dish for people who enjoy food. I have always enjoyed food, but what was my appetite compared with Lina's? Her queenliness melted, and a gentle bliss, an air of happy innocence took its place. Her teeth, her eyes, her glossy lips shone like a girl's. There are few beautiful women who can guzzle without loss of prestige. Lina did not push away her plate until she had emptied it four, five times. A little strawberry water-ice, a cup of coffee, and up she sprang, fastening a pair of castenets to her thumbs.

"Maria, to the piano with you. You others, zhove ziz table out of my way into zat corner!"

It would be hardly ten o'clock. Until two in the morning Caroline Otero would dance and sing—for her own enjoyment, she cared little for ours. From a handsome forty she became a lively seventeen. The bathwrap tossed aside, she danced in her petticoat, which was of brocaded silk with a flounce five metres round, the only garment essential to Spanish dancing. Soaked with sweat, her fine lawn chemise clung to her loins. Her moist skin gave off a delicate scent, a dusky scent, predominantly of sandalwood, that was more subtle than herself. There was nothing base in her violent and wholly selfish pleasure; it was born of a true passion for rhythm and music. She would snatch up her sauce-stained table-napkin and wipe herself vigorously, face, neck and damp armpits, then dance again, sing again: "Ziz one? D'you know it?" Her feet were not very light, but her face, tilted backward over her shoulders, the muscles of her waist rippling above the powerful loins, the savage, swaying furrow of her naked back could defy the harshest glare. A body that had defied sickness, ill-usage and the passage of time—a well-nourished body, sleek of sinew, bright of skin, amber by day, white by night—I have always told myself that I would, some day, with due care and detachment, describe it and its arrogant decline. We cannot paint a beloved face without passionately distorting it—and who speaks willingly of the things that belong to real love? But we can catch and hold—with words or with the brush—the crimson flush of dying leaves, the green of a meteor against the blue night, a moment of dawn, a catastrophe. Pictures which of themselves have no sense or depth, but which we invest with meaning or sharp foreboding—they bear for ever the stamp of a particular year, mark the end of a run of bad luck, or the culmination of a spell of prosperity. For that reason no one of us can ever swear that he has painted, contemplated, described in vain.

There was one man I never understood, the man who, all his life long, pretended to be poor. The pleasures he enjoyed were beyond compare. For not only did he dissemble the truth about his income—which is merely human—but he even borrowed from the poor themselves. He loved the tart flavour of the bailiff's visit and —like a sheep with a good thick fleece that goes through a thorn fence at the cost of a tuft or two—he would let them have a few worn-out flannel vests, an old pair of trousers and a handful of slightly frayed collars, the rest of his possessions being stored away safely under another name. No one was ever let into the secret of his hiding-places. He earned a reputation for extravagance at the least possible expense to himself and, when gambling at Monte Carlo, made no end of a show losing a few five franc plaques.

His constant cry—I know it only too well—was "Quick, dear, quick! There's not a sou in the house!" Quickly, indeed, his secretaries flew to the post-offices, laden with a copious correspondence—consisting entirely of express letter-cards—and quickly Pierre Veber, Jean de Tinan, Curnonsky, Boulestin, Passurf, Raymond Bouyer, Jean de la Hire, etc., knocked off chapters of this or that novel. Quickly, first Alfred Ernst, then Vuillermoz, André Hallays, Stan Gollestan, Claude Debussy, Vincent d'Indy himself, provided precious matter for the *Lettres de l'Ouvreuse*.[1] Quickly Eugène de Solenières and Aussaresses rattled off *Le Mariage de Louis XV*. Quickly, quickly I wrote the *Claudines* in four volumes, *Minne, Les Egarements de Minne*. At the *Retraite Sentimentale* I jibbed. And I don't think that anywhere in the course of these recollections, which I am setting down as they come, without deliberate order or plan—I don't think I shall be led into saying why. The names of his more recent collaborators are unknown to me. We, the veterans of the old gang—Pierre Veber, Vuillemoz, that excellent fellow "Cur", Prince of Gastronomes, Marcel Boulestin and myself—whenever we meet and talk of our duped and despoiled past, we always say: "In the days when we worked at *the factory*."

My life as a young woman began with this freebooter. A momentous encounter for a village girl! Before that—

---

[1] See Collection of the Princess de Polignac.
Translator's Note: Les Lettres de l'Ouvreuse, the title of a weekly article of musical criticism.

except for my parents' ruin, the money gone, the furniture sold by public auction—it had been roses, roses all the way. But what would I have done with everlasting roses?

The book that should be written is that man's life-story. The trouble is that no one ever really knew him. Three or four women still shudder when they hear his name—three or four whom I know personally. Now that he is dead their terror is gradually subsiding. While he was alive I must admit there were good reasons for it.

Quite a lot of us have our own little private picture of M. Willy. The people who did not see much of him talk of "that good fellow Willy". Those who had to do with him at all closely say nothing. Because of the many tales, the direct and indirect allusions, I am obliged to speak of him, although, as Tessa says, there are "nicer subjects of conversation". But his name is linked with a certain moment of time, with a particular case in modern literature, and with my name.

The personal appearance, the manner, a tone of voice, a turn of mind, are enough to disguise a human being utterly in the eyes of other human beings. How could we have guessed—I cannot do better than use the plural pronoun and take my place modestly in the crowd—how could we have realised that figures, figures first and foremost, haunted M. Willy and his fine mathematician's brow? Most of us refused to believe it. Figures were his greatest entertainment, the source of his deepest pleasures and of his gravest guilt. To count, to amass, to hoard—even in the flood of letters that have survived him, these are his chief concerns. The handwriting slants upward; it is extremely small, microscopic in fact, and the curious reader soon becomes as weary, deciphering it, as he is bored with the monotony of the text. The "Notes" are as dull as the letters themselves!

*"Sub. from L'Echo
53 marks 10 forwarded"*
*"Enter all this in the book, old chap.
To expenses:*

M.M. on account	*200 francs*
Hans Dichter	*50 —*
Félix Potin	*17 —*
August balance	*30 —*
Rates	*20 francs 50.*

*To Juliet for the housekeeping: 124 francs 50,
from which you must deduct the 94 francs she was
given by hand.
I have made a note of all this but had no time
to copy it into the book. Put it down! Put it down!
That postal order for a louis—have you entered it?
I can't trust that hare-brained memory of yours!
I think I made a note of the 40 francs sent to
Eisenhardt, but make sure, old chap."*

But what *book*? I have had account-books myself, like other people. The book that was constantly in M. Willy's mind, even, as you see, during his travels, was something very special, very private, indeed very secret. He was a tidy man and kept it with the utmost care, entrusting it, when he left home, to one, only, of his many secretaries. For all his love of order, the margins are sprinkled with minute calculations, figures as wee as midges, as grains of sand. One day, after my divorce, a yellowing sheet of paper, covered with such figures, slipped out of an old letter-rack that had been sent on to me. I picked it up. O wonder of wonders! It was a list of shares purchased by M. Willy, the soundest on the market.

I have hardly ever seen *the* book; it had fallen to pieces

by the time I glanced through it—a very common, cheap kind of ledger, long and rather narrow, bound in black cloth.

Figures, figures. . . . Where did you take me—I who paid so little heed to you? We had been married a year or a year and a half when M. Willy said to me: "You ought to put down what you remember of your board-school days. Don't be shy of the spicy bits. I might make something of it. Money's short."

These last words, which were his daily *leitmotif*—a theme developed with unfailing fantasy for thirteen years—alarmed me less than the first. For I had just recovered from a long and very serious illness that had left me sluggish in mind and body. But having found and bought, at a local paper-shop, a number of copy-books similar to those I had used at school, I set to work. The heavy grey-ruled pages, the vertical red line of the margins, the black cover and its inset medallion and ornamental title, *Le Calligraphe*, re-awakened the urge, a sort of itch in my fingers, to do an 'imposition', to fulfil a prescribed task. A well-remembered water-mark in the thick, laid paper, took me back six years. Diligently, with complete indifference, perched at the corner of the desk, the window behind me, one shoulder hunched and my knees crossed, I wrote.

When I had finished, I gave my husband a manuscript that was closely-written and did not overrun the margins. He read it through and said: "I was wrong. It's no use at all."

Relieved, I returned to the divan, to my cat, my books, my new friends, to the life I tried to make pleasant, that I did not know was unhealthy.

A THIRD floor in the Rue Jacob, between two courtyards. One of the courtyards faced the north and the Rue Visconti, so that I had, at least, a glimpse of old tiled roofs to remind me of the tiles of Burgundy.

No sun. Three living rooms, a small, dark study, a kitchen on the other side of the landing—all this for fourteen hundred francs a year. In the square drawing-room was a salamander stove, and in the recess where I had set out my tub, my basins and my ewers, a gas fire. It was almost a poor man's flat, yet its white doors were early nineteenth century and still had their little carved wreaths and garlands, now half clogged with paint. I had not chosen it. On the day I saw it first it was empty, and I felt that I was only half awake. The last tenant had lived there for fifty years, long enough to complete a most singular form of decoration. The doors, the ornaments on the doors, the cornices, the skirtings, the niche for the porcelain stove in the dining-room, the sham wood panels, the shelves of the cupboards, the window frames and a large surface of the walls themselves, were covered with tiny diamond-shaped confetti of many colours, cut out and glued on by hand, one by one.

"I understood from the gentleman himself," the concierge confided to me in a low, reverent voice, "that there were more than two hundred and seventy-five thousand pieces. I call that work."

Work such as you do in nightmares. The thought of living in these rooms, in the presence of walls that had witnessed so secret a madness, so evil a joy, appalled me. And then I forgot about it. I was only a young bride.

No light, no air, the dark enchantment that sometimes lingers in places that have crushed and stifled many souls. The little flat must, I think, have been profoundly melancholy. And yet, to me, it seemed agreeable. What it is to have known worse! I had gone to it from another lodging, M. Willy's bachelor establishment, a quaking, echoing garret, at the top of one of the houses on the quays, that shivered at every passing bus and lorry. I have never been able to forget that attic and its murky, rattling double windows. Painted in bottle green and chocolate brown, filled with unspeakably sordid cardboard files, soaked in a sort of horrible office gloom, it looked uninhabited, utterly forsaken. The draughts crept over the creaking boards; their slightest breath brought forth, out of the black shadows, from under the sagging springs of the bed, a grey snow, a drift of flakes born, as some frail nests are born, of a thread, a hair, woven with dust as light and soft as down. Heaps of yellowing newspapers occupied the chairs; German postcards were strewn more or less everywhere, celebrating the attractions of underclothes, socks, ribboned drawers and buttocks. The master of the house would have strongly objected to any attempt on my part to remedy the disorder.

It was a relief to get away, every morning, from these indecent surroundings. The place had been adapted solely to the use, the careless convenience of a dissolute bachelor, and I welcomed the daylight that took me from it. I welcomed the daylight also for its own sake, because it drew me out of bed and into the open air. And because I was hungry. By half-past eight or thereabouts, M. Willy and I were crossing the bridge. Ten minutes' walk took us to the humble milkshop where the blue-smocked packers from *La Belle Jardinière* kept up their strength, as we did, on rolls dipped in pale mauve chocolate.

Judging from various incidents that stand out sharply in a haze of unhappy memories, it would appear that M. Willy and I lived very poorly. It is quite possible, I may say probable. I remember that "Sido", my mother, came to Paris for a few days in the winter of 1894, or 1895— she always stayed at the Hôtel du Palais Royal—and found that I had no outdoor coat of any kind against the bitter weather. She said nothing. She gave her son-in-law a look out of her keen, wide eyes, and took me off to the *Magasins du Louvre* to buy a black top-coat, trimmed with 'Mongolian' fur that cost a hundred and twenty-five francs and seemed to me sumptuous. The very young are not deeply affected by certain forms of hardship. The incongruous, too, often scarcely touches them. The picture comes back to me suddenly of a heap of gold shining on the black-painted deal writing-table and its red baize cover—a mass of gold louis that M. Willy had spilt there out of his pockets.

"Take as much of it," he said, "as you can hold in both hands. You'll count up afterwards."

I counted eight hundred and twenty francs. Coined gold is a pretty metal; it has a fine, clear ring, and warms pleasantly to the touch.

"I hope," said M. Willy, "that you won't want any more housekeeping money now for at least two months."

It seemed quite natural to go about with an empty purse, as I had done before my marriage; it never occurred to me, either, that I might have lived more comfortably. After the morning's cup of lilac chocolate,

I would hurry back to my dark quarters. I did not realise that in their strange gloom I was gradually losing strength, that the life was ebbing from a vigorous country girl, brought up on the wealth that the countryside granted in those days to the poor; milk at twopence a quart, fruit and vegetables, butter at sevenpence a pound, eggs at sevenpence ha'penny the dozen, chestnuts, walnuts . . . In Paris I was never hungry. I hid in my corner, chiefly because I did not wish to know Paris. The town filled me with dread, and after ten months of marriage I already had most excellent reasons for fearing it. A book, hundreds of books, low, airless rooms, sweets instead of meat, an oil lamp instead of sunshine—and always the persistent, absurd hope to which I clung: this great evil, this city life, could not last; it would be cured miraculously, by my death and resurrection, by a shock that would restore me to my mother's house, to the garden, and wipe out everything that marriage had taught me.

Is it hard to understand how to have gone from a village home to the life I led after 1894 was an adventure so serious that it could bring a child of twenty to despair? Despair or a wild intoxication. It is true that, at first, ridden by youth and ignorance, I had known intoxication—a guilty rapture, an atrocious, impure, adolescent impulse. There are many scarcely nubile girls who dream of becoming the show, the plaything, the licentious masterpiece of some middle-aged man. It is an ugly dream that is punished by its fulfilment, a morbid thing, akin to the neuroses of puberty, the habit of eating chalk and coal, of drinking mouthwash, of reading dirty books and sticking pins into the palm of the hand.

So I was punished, quickly and thoroughly. One day, dressed in my handsome, hundred-and-twenty-five franc coat, my serpent of hair bound with a new ribbon, I took a cab to the Rue Bochard-de-Saron and rang the bell of a minute, mezzanine-floor flat. Anonymous letters often tell the truth. There, in fact, were M. Willy and Mlle Charlotte Kinceler, not in bed but sitting in front of—yes!—an open account book. M. Willy was holding the pencil. I listened to the pulse beating in my tonsils, and the two lovers stared, astounded, at the pale young provincial with the long hair, her plait coiled round her neck, her fringe curling on her forehead. What could I say? A dark little woman—four foot ten, to be exact—was watching me, a pair of scissors grasped tightly in her hand; a word, a movement, and she would have flown at my face. Was I afraid? No, I wasn't afraid. Violence, catastrophe, the hope of disaster, blood, a sudden shriek—at twenty, if you look into yourself, you can see tragic landscapes any day that are far finer than that. I should say that neither Mlle Kinceler nor I seemed in the least put out, whereas M. Willy sat mopping his brow, which was vast, powerful and pink.

"You've come to fetch me?" he said.

I glanced uncertainly at Mlle Kinceler and my husband, at my husband and Mlle Kinceler, and found nothing better than to say, in my politest drawing-room manner:

"Why yes. Don't you think . . . ?"

He rose, pushed me in front of him, hustled me out of the front door with almost magical celerity. In the street I felt a little proud of having shown no fear, uttered no threats. But I was sorry I had not heard Mlle Kinceler's voice. And above all I was taken up, bitterly absorbed, by what I had seen: the neat, tidy little flat, a sunny window, a general air of ease and familiarity, the half-folded table with its American-cloth cover, a cage of canaries, the corner of a large bed just showing in the next room, the shining brasses and enamels of a tiny kitchen, the rather corpulent man seated sideways on a caned chair, the little firebrand of a woman grasping her scissors—and the intruder, the girl with the long plait, silent and slender in her ready-made coat.

I could hear my husband's short, agitated breathing. From time to time he removed his flat-brimmed top hat and wiped his forehead. He could not make out what it all meant, my arrival, my silence, my oddly restrained behaviour. Nor could I. Later, I understood that through the strangeness and the shock, the depths of my amazement and indeed of my despair, I had been able to think quickly, to make up my mind at once that whatever happened I must hide the truth from "Sido". I kept my word.

I was not able to deceive her completely; she had eyes that could see through walls. But for thirteen years I did my best to make her think me altogether happy. It was not easy, especially at first. When I went to stay with her at Châtillon-Coligny, there was always one moment that I looked forward to with dread. The early hours of my visit were simple enough. Although the house was small and poor, very different from the big house at Saint-Sauveur where I was born, merely to be in it, to live a country life again, gave me back my fondness for laughter, for chattering and asking questions, for driving in the wheezy De Dion with my doctor brother and waiting for him by the farmhouse gates. On the evening of my arrival I used to tell my mother of the new people I had met, describe Catulle Mendès and Gustave Charpentier, Judith Gautier's black cat and her green lizard, Courteline. . . . But soon the moment would come, I could feel it drawing near, when my brother's weariness, the exhaustion of fifteen hours' ceaseless rounds, must take his white face and tired limbs to rest, the moment when my father must enjoy the sleep that comes so swiftly to ageing men, the moment, the beloved hour when I would be alone with my mother. Stretched out, the hot water bottle at my feet, I had to watch her sit down in the dilapidated armchair beside my bed, her cheeks flushed with pleasure at the sight of me and exasperation at her own fatigue: "Oh, that back . . . that left leg . . . that neck of mine!"

She would have nothing of her ills. Her way of speaking of them was a rejection, a denial of their existence. She had a gesture, too, that seemed to cast them off, as though she were flinging back a cloak that was too hot, or a mane of long thick hair.

"Now tell me, tell me . . ."

Her questions, her eyes searched me with alarming penetration. But I was her daughter and already proficient at the game. So I chattered on of Paris, told her a hundred more tales of the hateful town I knew so little. I talked about plays and concerts, I kept a harsh grip on myself, in terror of that last, that greatest danger: 'If she tucks me in, if, before tucking me in, she takes me in her arms, if I smell her soft hair and feel it on my cheek, if she chooses to call me her "lovely sunshine", then all is lost.'

An hour later she called me her "lovely sunshine", pressed her thin, silky hair against my cheek and tucked the bedclothes under the mattress. I lay stiff and attentive, making no movement, saying no word, allowing nothing, nothing to escape me except a mumble of feigned drowsiness, a pretence of half-sleep. At the cost of such self-denial I got safely to the time when "Sido" would cry: "Eleven o'clock!" take the cat under her arm, pick up the oil lamp with her free hand and leave me until the morrow.

I have never been able to cry with ease, decency and fitting emotion. Tears are as grievous to me as vomiting; they swell my nostrils and distort my mouth into an ugly square shape; they leave me with stiffened, aching ribs and hideously puffed eyelids. I cry as badly, as painfully as a man. But you can do away with tears if you put your mind to it; after I had been through a thorough training, I scarcely ever indulged in them. I have friends of thirty years standing who have never seen my eyes damp. "What? *You* cry?" they exclaim and stare at me under or over their spectacles, scanning my face, trying to imagine the traces of weeping, there beside the nose, there by the corner of the mouth. "*You* cry! Why how absurd!" They burst out laughing, and so do I, for after all to cry in public is a sort of incontinence that does not give you time, if it comes upon you suddenly, to run away and hide behind the nearest wall. I detest tears—perhaps because I have found them so very hard to conquer.

I saw Charlotte Kinceler again, later on. So did you, if you ever went to Brieux's *Les Hannetons*. "Lotte of Montmartre", daughter of a drink-sodden Communard, tempted Brieux, who wrote this play round her and chose Polaire for the chief part. Lotte seduced Lucien Guitry, dazzled Jules Lemaître and many others of the famous or prominent men who watched and listened to her shyly. Sometimes they slept with her, ritually as it were, hierophants of the new cult of which she was the first young priestess, of the new-born convention that was Montmartre. She was fresh-looking and tainted and could already—even to my inexperienced eyes—be suspected of directing and controlling the natural outflow of her talents, of turning their deep, spontaneous, lusty streams into artificial channels. But she had a long way to go before her dwarf's conceit could become tedious, her crippled urchin's wit irksome. To Jules Lemaître, dining with her and M. Willy at the austere 'Foyot's', her prattle was like a chattering of Polynesian natives. He bent over her hands, her extraordinarily small feet, and marvelled. His guest spread her little claws out over the table.

"Five and a quarter I take," she said proudly, "and kids' size in shoes. My sister's the same. It's in the family."

"So you have a sister?"

"I should say so. Madame Ducroquet. She's a *demi-mondaine*."

"Oh!" exclaimed Lemaître, "you should have brought her!"

She shook her head loftily.

"Can't be done. She swipes the silver."

"She—what?" Lemaître enquired, wondering. "Wipes the silver? I don't see anything so very strange in that. Of course it depends where you are dining . . ."

"No!" cried Lotte. "She snaffles it, I tell you!"

Lemaître flushed under the reproof.

"She——? I'm sorry, but I really don't understand."

Disheartened, Lotte appealed to M. Willy, whom she commonly addressed as "Kiki". With a sideway glance at the ingenuous Lemaître:

"Kiki!" she protested. "You told me he was clever!"

At this the gentle playwright beamed. His shrewd, kind eyes dwelt, enchanted, upon Lotte.

"What a joy she is! If only one could get her on the stage. . . ."

The native of Montmartre gave him her renewed

esteem in a glowing, black and white look, veiled in dense, Oriental lashes.

"Oh! but I want to! Besides, I've got an idea for a play —a real play, none of your rotten funny pieces; they're all my eye; sloppy nonsense I call them—a *real* play. I'd act in it. Shall I tell it you? It's like this . . . I'd be a young married woman. My husband's a soaker, same as father. He drinks half the time and the rest of the time of course he cats. . . . I'm ever so unhappy. A bloke comes along who's rich and handsome and everything. He makes up to me. 'You get a divorce,' he says, 'and your life will be one long, sweet dream.' That looks a bit different to me, naturally! So one evening when I get back from work——"

"What work?" asked Lemaître.

"What work! What work!" Lotte repeated irritably. "What's he interrupting me for with his 'What work!'? I train fleas or I take in sewing. . . . So one evening when I get back from work I begin to cry. 'Ah!' I say to myself, 'the die is cast! I'll chuck the stinker and find true happiness.' But what do I see when I open the door? My husband's come home drunk and vomited everywhere! Vomited over the counterpane, vomited over the rug. Vomited over the curtains and the fern and the china flower-pot. So I kneel down and fold my hands and say——" She put her hands together and raised her eyes until only their whites were visible: "I say: 'This is where my duty lies. . . .' Well? What do you think of that?"

"I—er—of course——" stammered Lemaître. "To tell you the truth I had pictured you rather in comic parts."

"Comic!!!"

Standing up, and scarcely taller than he was sitting in

his chair, she blazed at him. She turned to M. Willy, who was finding the party far from dull.

"*My good man*, you'll be kind enough in future not to invite me with flats like this. Stupid I wouldn't mind so much, but heartless—that I *can't* forgive. I'd sooner go home. And d'you want to know what I think? If you pay the bill, I'll say you're as big a bloody fool as he is!"

Lotte and I became, not friendly, but curious of one another, courteous, like duellists after a fight. She confessed to M. Willy that she had been much struck by my composure. "She looks a bit English, your wife, and she wears her hat too far back on her head. And those little curls on her forehead—they make you think of village weddings. All the same, when she came in that day she looked as if the place belonged to her. . . ." For my part I admired in Lotte qualities that I could never achieve as long as I lived: glibness of tongue, a miraculously nimble body, and complete omniscience. When she opened her herbalist's shop in the Rue Pauquet and I went there to buy my boracic vaseline, my handful of camomile tea, we faced each other again, and I did my best, a little over-sweetly, to win her favour. I was meek, I listened with extreme attention, making it plain that, from her, I had everything to learn. She expanded under the flattery. Sometimes, not to be behindhand in good manners, she would call on me, very much the lady in a short astrakhan coat, a great bunch of Parma violets tucked in at her waist, and a chenille-spotted veil stretched over her Peke's nose. One day, on arrival, she opened her fur coat, scented with Corylopsis, and drew from her bodice the edge of a chemise in finest handkerchief lawn, encrusted with Mechlin lace butterflies. M. Willy whistled admiringly.

"My word! Where did you get that?"

"A chap," said Lotte. "Three days. But I've done with him. What with the mug he had and a name like a bad joke—I slung him out."

"What name?"

"Oh! a name—what was it? Richard Lenoir. No, wait a minute, that's wrong. Edmond Blanc."[1]

There is nothing strange, I think, in my lingering over memories of Lotte Kinceler. She, who lived such a little while, taught me a great deal. With her came my first doubts of the man I had given myself to so trustfully, and the end of my girlhood, that uncompromising, exalted, absurd estate. From her I got my first notions of tolerance and concealment and the possibility of coming to terms with an enemy. Concentration, humility—it was an instructive time. Lotte sold me her zinc ointment as though it were worth its weight in gold, but I was still the gainer. In her parlour, behind the shop, I drank lime-flower tea, served on a fringed table-cloth, and lost my foolish belief that because she had deceived me with my husband, Lotte had no object in life but to deceive me. The shop-bell tinkled. She would run forward to greet her customers, to recommend this or that type of preservative, to enquire into the condition of a captious bowel, to weigh dried wormwood for a "panic-stricken" mother. To all of them, men and women alike, she spoke the same admirable language, the language of the fortune-teller and the ancient oracles and the old wives who gather and brew simples in the villages. Black as hell, delicately slim, her waist laced to strangulation-point, she would draw herself up with the vigour and the majesty of a serpent and lift a childish forefinger to admonish and to soothe the angry parent.

[1] *Translator's Note:* Edmond Blanc was a well-known racing man, immensely rich.

"When Nature has spoken, Madame, there is nothing to be said. The sharpest of us have only to bow down. Nature has spoken in your daughter, Madame. So she's in trouble—that's Fate. But now," she added, "we shall have to do something about it, shan't we? Nature does not seek the death of the sinner. . . ."

Reaching up towards the crimson ear of a young male customer, she would whisper with precision and authority, the perfect saleswoman, smiling in a manner that allowed of no misunderstanding. The small parcels fetched and spread out on the counter, she would end with these convincing words: "This, my dear Sir, cannot be called a measure of precaution. It is an ornament, a real ornament."

Evening came, and she threw off her white overall, put on a hat, a coat that was invariably in the best taste, and I would leave her, full of envy for the four-foot-ten princess with the button nose, the dazzling teeth and eyes, who was going out to dine in literary Bohemia.

A short time before her death, she got the idea of confession and Communion into her head, she who had never thought of baptism. She went to the confessional as she would have swallowed a drink in a public-house on a very thirsty day. She had to do with a priest no doubt of the very highest genius, a ponderous, rough man whom she saw three or four times and to whom she succumbed instantly. His face was scarcely visible to her through the wooden grating, but she could hear his voice and his heavy gasping, smell his sour breath. She seemed aware of who knows what eagerness, what urge to die, and wrote "Kiki" confused letters, darkly foreboding, slashed with light: "I've been to *that place* again, to see that priest chap. Oh! Kiki! I can't help it—it's the most extraordinary thing—it's sending me potty. He sweats, he stinks, he belches—and he is bringing me to God!"

M. Willy kept the letters carefully, filing them with all his other letters in a box-file of the sort that has a punching apparatus at the side and makes three holes in the margins. But Lotte could not wait for the miracle that was drawing near and disturbing her so much. One afternoon of stifling summer rain she went into her backshop parlour and shot herself through the mouth. She was twenty-six years old and had saved money.

THE memories of my first and second years of marriage are clear and fantastic, like the impressions that dwell in the mind after some confused dream in which every detail, beneath its apparent incoherence, is plainly and fatally symbolic. But I was twenty-one and kept forgetting the symbols.

The spells woven by a voluntary seclusion are not all evil. Before the Kinceler incident came to warn me of my danger and arouse a taste for survival and self-defence, I had found it very hard to accept that there should be so marked a difference between the condition of a maid and the condition of a wife, between life in the country and life in Paris, between happiness—or at all events the illusion of happiness—and its absence, between love and the laborious, exhausting sexual pastime.

I had certain compensations. I enjoyed the prolonged, sheltered leisure that prisoners enjoy and the rest that is allowed to invalids. A child that is wounded, or in plaster, and is compelled to lie up, will soon become accustomed to its helplessness. It will arrange and furnish its bed and grow fond of it. My bed, my refuge, my worldly goods were my youth and my dislike of people, my hatred of the town all round me, and a desperate determination to suffer from love rather than renounce it or complain. I had books and the listless, unceasing poison of the salamander stove that burned without interruption from September till June. I had my new men friends but no woman friend. Girls like the company of mature men but, secretly, it depresses them. My husband was fifteen years older than I was. Pierre Veber, M. Willy's witness at our marriage ceremony, was twenty-eight, but he had gone off immediately after the wedding, to join the young people that his own fresh, slim, whispering, witty youth deserved, nay demanded. He used to come, sometimes, to the Rue Jacob, and I would breathe the air he brought in with him, his well-groomed young man's scent; I would look at him with pleasure and surprise and never dream that I could possibly have desired him. Meanwhile M. Willy's bald head glistened under the lamp, and a little further off sat Paul Masson, our melancholy, humorous daily guest, pulling at his little pointed beard, already going grey. My other friend, Marcel Schwob, had nothing young at thirty but his passion for all human knowledge, his vehement manner, his aggressive, sudden outbursts of brilliance.

Between my two unseasonable companions I was never bored. Every day, to beguile my ceaseless craving to be with her, to live by her side for ever, I wrote a letter to "Sido". I let myself sink back, sink down into a half dream, a half light, a vagueness, the habit of silence, the dim pleasure of being pale and a little breathless, of spreading my long, heavy hair—long, long as myself—over a trailing Renaissance teagown.

I could brush and plait it, but in other ways I was awkward and could not dress the long hair that my mother's hands had never coiled and pinned about my head. If I felt cold, I unplaited it and grew warm, wrapped in its smooth cape. At night I plaited it again and dreamed of snakes when the ends of the braids caught between my toes.

In 1895—or was it 1894?—my father-in-law presided at the Polytechnique Annual Ball, and I went there on his arm, dressed in a grand, sea-green frock with a lace cape, the masterpiece of a Batignolles seamstress. People stared a good deal at the *jeune fille* in the green gown that was no greener than herself—I was extremely ill—with the ribbon knotted on her forehead and the great serpent of hair stirring in the folds of her train.

That wan *jeune fille* was near death, yet did not die. She gave a lot of trouble to Dr Jullien, the great Saint-Lazare physician, who looked after her for two months and scolded her gently. "Get well, my dear! Help me a little! I am trying so hard to cure you and you do nothing!" There is always a moment in the lives of the very young when death seems as natural and as attractive as life, and I was hesitating. How could I, in any case, have complained of an illness that brought me back "Sido"?

For she came, bringing with her a light array of black satinette frocks for the day time and white bed-jackets for the night; she came when Dr Jullien wrote to tell her that he would probably not save me. She hid everything from me and everybody else, nursed me with a laughing tenderness, slept in the black dining-room. All I noticed was that she seemed flushed, from time to time, and out of breath. No doubt she toiled, day and night, dragging me away from the threshold she would not have me cross. And so I got well, and "Sido" hastened back to where my father waited and pined—though not without my having noticed the singular, invariable coolness she displayed towards the man she always called—am I not right to copy her?—Monsieur Willy.

Never having been through another serious illness, I have not known that astonishing state again, a weakness so great that it left me no strength for deep suffering. I remember that I was in bed for sixty days and that I was gay and laughed easily. I took care of my face and hands and confided my feet and hair to "Sido".

But I needed water as a dry plant needs rain. I begged for baths, which my merciful doctor allowed me, rather unwillingly, every five or six days. Once a week or so the bath was brought up, just as it would have been in the eighteenth century. A hairy and muscular herald appeared first, cowled in a red copper bath that must surely have been used by Marat. The steaming buckets came next; the inside of the bath was shrouded in a coarse linen sheet, and they were poured out. My mother's hands wound my plaits round my head, four arms lifted me up, I was deposited in the hot water. I lay there, shivering with fever, weakness, the wish to cry, the exhaustion of bodily misery. My teeth continued to chatter for a long while after I had been dried and put back to bed and could amuse myself watching the bath-attendants taking out the water, first by the bucketful, finally in little saucepans. The copper sarcophagus went its way, Juliette, the little maid, mopped up the traces of its passage, and Paul Masson would come in to pay me a visit, or else Marcel Schwob, or—more rarely—Madame Arman de Caillavet. Anatole France's celebrated friend was good to me; she felt sorry, I think, for an invalid so young, so defenceless, condemned to lie so long on a gloomy polished walnut bed, in a room where nothing spoke of comfort, of personal choice, of love. She would bring peaches and lay them by my pillow, or a pineapple, or a large, knotted, foulard scarf full of sweets. A high lace ruff rose above the collar of her sable cloak; her toque was a bird not unlike herself—an owl, beloved of Minerva—that crowned her with its curved beak and outstretched wings. She never stayed long, yet her broad, well-shaped hand, her peremptory and slightly gasping voice, her overpowering scent gave me a brief, vivid sense of ease.

Sitting faithfully beside my bed, Marcel Schwob would open a book of American or English tales, Mark Twain, Jerome K. Jerome, Dickens, or *Moll Flanders*—which he had not translated at that time—and would read to me, so that I should lie still, so that I should bear with my illness and the round, black blistering plasters that bit into my hollow belly, symmetrically, so many on each side. I took the wealth poured out by this excellent scholar—he was much greater than his work—as a matter of course. He was already weak and walked with difficulty, yet he climbed our three storeys twice, three times a day, talked to me, translated for me, wasted his time on me with superb generosity. And I was not in the least astonished; I treated him as if he belonged to me. At twenty, you accept munificent gifts in the royal manner, as though they were your due.

The portrait that Sacha Guitry drew of Marcel Schwob is the only portrait that was ever like him. Angular eyelids, their corners pointed as arrowheads, a pale and terribly blazing eye, lips that withheld their dagger-secret, polishing it, sharpening it, exquisitely enjoying it —never can a more formidable countenance have concealed, as with a ceremonial mask, a battle mask, what was to me, for three years, the very face of friendship.

My other friend and daily visitor was less striking in appearance and manner, if no less mysterious. He was grey of feature, inconspicuous and unforgettable; his little beard was like dry hay, his laugh thin and grating, his glance that of a bad priest. He was addicted to puns and hoaxes, which he worked out as elaborately as the subtlest crimes. The few crumbs of writing that he left were signed "Lemice-Térieux": the *Thoughts of a Yogi*, a Catalogue of the "Salon de la Nationale", composed with incredible ingenuity entirely of puns prodigiously contrived to include the name of the artist and the title of the picture. His patience and his great culture allowed him, occasionally, to indulge in jokes of a sort that could truly be called criminal and threatened the peace of Europe; an 'Early Diary' of Bismarck's, written by Paul Masson, brought France and Germany within an ace of war. "A little sooner, a little later", said this monomaniac.

He had been a magistrate at Chandernagor, and had, in that capacity, delivered judgements of which the remarkable "reasons adduced" had not got as far as Europe; he said himself that "it was a pity . . ." But a full story of the expulsion of the Jesuits, sent to *Le Figaro* and printed in that paper, stirred such disquiet in the breasts of pious Frenchmen that the Government, taken aback, ordered an enquiry. Need I say with what zeal, what scrupulous care Paul Masson conducted it? The lengthiest and most detailed of the reports bear witness to the fact, proving conclusively that there had been no Jesuits in French India since the reign of Louis XV.

His looks and general air made you think of the evil spirits who visit villages and whose business is to seduce the girls, turn the Lord of the Manor into a wolf and the virtuous attorney into a vampire. He sometimes gave his address but never opened his door. I believe that he had kept the habits of his colonial-magistrate days and still smoked opium, but I have no proof of this whatever. All I am sure of is the affection and probably the compassion that he felt for me when he understood the circumstances of my new life and saw me waste away so grievously. As for his passion for mystification, I believe that it was to him what to another man would be a vice, or an art.

It should be said that the practical joke was in high

favour at that time, enjoying a popularity that now seems incomprehensible. More recently we have had the 'surprise party', which is a gross and fortunately dangerous form of adventure. But the years 1890-1895 had their official, their licensed 'wags'; Vivier, Sapeck, led to Salis, foretold and prepared the way for Allais and Jarry. With the decline of leisure, practical-joking changed, became over-subtle, over-delicate and finally died, leaving the throne to heirs who were able to take material advantage of a gift that their predecessors had exploited for its own sake.

A disregard for money, a malicious sense of the future are the distinguishing features of a "Lemice-Térieux". Paul Masson wrought in silence, for posterity. He was on the staff of the Bibliothèque Nationale Catalogue and seemed to live very simply, to have all he needed. But everything he allowed us to know of him was an empty pretence, a sham, destined to mislead, to keep up an illusion.

When at last, and most surprisingly, I got almost well and went with M. Willy to Belle-Ile-en-Mer, Paul Masson came with us, clad in the suit he invariably wore, which was of black cloth, bound with mohair braid.[1] He did not seem strong, yet he was never tired, always ready to follow me and my lively young exuberance that every day of sunshine and salt water made livelier. The positively Mediterranean riches of the island amazed and enchanted us. Terraces and vines, fig-trees as plentiful as in Italy, lizards in grey traceries upon the rocks, blue and pink sails upon the sea. The yearly tide of women had already come, the Bigoudines, bright as scarabs in their caps and glittering dresses, who were engaged to prepare and

[1] The character of Masseau, in *L'Entrave*, written many years later, was taken from him.

cook the season's catch of sardines. When the fish were delayed the girls waited, filling in time by a determined pursuit of every creature in trousers.

"Don't you want someone?" they used to call after my friend.

"What for?"

"To sleep with you...."

He made a forked sign at them with his fingers, and they fled in terror, their rich skirts wafting towards us, as they ran, a lingering smell of rotten fish. Together we wanderered over the island, from Kervilaouen to the wild *Mer Sauvage*, from Sauzon to the Poulains, leaving M. Willy respectfully to his writing, which was extraordinarily copious, at least in its epistolary form, each long hour of solitude and quiet producing a huge volume of letters and telegrams that might well have alarmed a young wife. But I was already learning to look the other way.

I made Paul Masson come with me to the old fortress on the Pointe des Poulains that Sarah Bernhardt bought later on. At the Pointe the sands shone mauve in the sunlight, strewn with a dust of crumbled rubies; I collected the biggest I could find and lost them again. For the first time in my life I tasted, I touched the salt, the sand, the seaweed, the moist and fragrant bed of the ebbing tide, the glistening fish. The Atlantic air soothed, lulled the memories of my long illness and the habit of active thought.

To the west of the island the *Mer Sauvage* came racing in—"all the way from America!" I would say with deep consideration. The constant thunder of the waves, the galloping manes of foam that drove the wind, the stones and sands before them, made all talk between Paul Masson and myself impossible. From time to time squalls would come up over the restless water, bringing rain that could be as harsh as hail. When this happened I used to take shelter with my silent companion in the caves and hollows of the rocks. I was quite happy to wait there patiently and watch the sea grow pale on the horizon. On one such occasion I remember Paul Masson turning up the braided collar of his coat and sitting himself down on a stool of purple granite. The afternoon was blue with low clouds, milky with rain. He drew from his pocket a small writing-case, a pen that had a cap on it and a little bundle of cardboard dockets on each of which he proceeded to write a few words in a round, copperplate hand.

"What are you doing, Paul?"

His eyes, narrow between their creased lids, did not look up from the cards before him.

"I am working. I am working at my job. I am on the staff of the Library Catalogue. I am writing out titles."

I was already fairly credulous; I gasped with surprise and admiration.

"Oh! And you can do that from memory!"

He pointed his little clock-maker's beard at me.

"From memory? What would be the good of that? I am doing something much more useful. I have observed that the Library is singularly lacking in Latin and Italian works of the fifteen century. Also in German manuscripts. Also in the private correspondence of royalty. And there are many other small lacunae. No doubt luck or scholarship will soon remedy the shortage but until that occurs I propose to provide the titles of these extremely interesting works . . . they should, they ought to have been written. In this way I shall at least save the honour of the Catalogue, of the Kha—talogue. . . ."

"But why?" I objected naïvely, "if the books don't exist?"

He waved an airy hand. "Ah!" said he. "I can't do everything...."

I have written a good deal about Paul Masson because he astonished me and because, when he died, I lost my first friend, the first friend of my young womanhood. Later, it came into my mind that he had grown very fond of me. From that, to supposing that I deserved his fondness was only a step: a solitary man, a prematurely aged bachelor who had travelled much, his affection did something to restore the confidence of a child deceived, betrayed as soon as married, secluded in her semblance of a home and obstinately resolved to hide there and reign over two friends and a cat. Thanks to him I came to value a little more highly what there was in me that was unusual, attractive, desolate, secret. Outwardly I was all silence and disquiet, a sovereign ruling and moving in the shadows, followed by her long tresses, fed on nuts and bananas like a monkey in a cage. If Paul Masson, in whom M. Willy sometimes confided, suffered from what he knew and was fearful for me, at least he never hinted at it by a single, dishonourable word.

His death was a classic example of a humorist's end: standing on the banks of the Rhine, he pressed a pad soaked in ether to his face until his legs gave way. He fell and was drowned in a foot of water.

W̱ʜᴀᴛ is known as the Bohemian life has always suited me about as badly as a hat trimmed with ostrich feathers or a pair of earrings. I do not mean the sort of 'Bohemia' that I organised for myself when the time came. That Bohemia would have given points for hard work and almost finical punctuality to any storekeeper's staff.

M. Willy still believed in the other, traditional Bohemian life and occasionally induced me to go with him and taste its pungent, commonplace flavour. But I had no gift for it, no fitting gaiety, and presently refused to follow. It was quite enough that I should have to spend half the night in a corner of the *Echo de Paris* Editorial, waiting for the proofs of the *Lettres de l'Ouvreuse*. The weariness of sitting on a bench, dangling my legs and swaying with sleep; the weariness of reading and re-reading, until I knew them by heart, all the clippings, bulls, printers' errors, absurd non seqs. that had been cut out of the newspapers and pinned on the walls; the weariness of pursuing a half-dream through the banks of smoke that moved slowly, heavily about lampshades scorched by the gas, roughly patched with yellowing paper; the weariness of not having had supper, the weariness of having had supper—the impression of so much weariness lingers in my nostrils as a smell of tobacco, of printer's ink and of the beer that a waiter brought in, the handles of five tankards hooked in the fingers of one hand. How strange those old editorial offices were, haunts of intellectual activity where nothing respected, protected, promoted thought! Every man seemed bent on provoking his neighbour. Reporters banged doors, sub-editors shouted at the tops of their voices, men on the news-in-brief columns came back, dripping, from the police-stations. No one was cheerful, dignified, young, or made the least effort to appear so.

I used to wake up with the arrival of Courteline or of Catulle Mendès. What a power it is to have no need of solitude! Mendès started writing instantly. He wrote while he talked, while he drank, while he smoked. As time grew short and zero hour drew near, old Simond emerged from his office and fidgeted about him anxiously. A herculean page-setter, yellow-eyed and half naked, with tightly curling hair and the face of a stoker, appeared, stepping stealthily. Slow and silent-footed, he would plant himself in front of Simond and hold out the piece of string, marked with filthy tallies, that he carried round his neck. "I've *that* much too much", he would say, or: "I've *that* much too little", and would then stand and wait, unmoved and implacable, until the cursing had died down.

Voluble as ever, white and soft as wax, Mendès continued to write. Courteline complained and argued. His bat-like voice rasped your ears, scraped at the plaster walls. Luminous young women came and sat in Catulle's shadow. Still writing, he greeted them with complicated and caressing epithets: "Hummingbird that alights upon a twig yet does not bend it . . ." "White loveliness that puts the snow to shame . . ." "Basket overflowing with treasure . . ."

He was not always so flowery, so inflated with languor. It happened one day, after we had lunched with him, M.

Willy and I, and had drunk his richly aromatic coffee—he always prepared it himself—that M. Willy went out of the room for a moment and Catulle turned to me sharply:

"You wrote the '*Claudines*', didn't you? That's all right, that's all right! I'm not asking questions, you needn't overdo the bashfulness. . . . In—in I don't know how long—in twenty years, in thirty years perhaps, people will find out. And then you'll see what it means for a writer to have created a type. You don't realise it now. Oh! it's a big thing! Certainly it's a big thing! But it's a sort of punishment too, a guilt that follows you everywhere, that sticks to your skin—a reward that becomes intolerable, that you want to spew up. . . . You can't get away from it, you've created a type."

Whereupon M. Willy came back and Catulle landed, without a break, lightly and easily in the middle of his favourite anti-semitic paradox: "Name me one Jew! One single Jew who was a creative genius!" When somebody once said to him: "And what about Spinoza?" he twisted out of it rather weakly: "Spinoza? Hum—— I'm not too sure about his mother."

But I have often thought of Catulle's prediction. He spoke of twenty years, thirty years; I am writing in 1935 and have this moment received a letter from a shirt- and blouse-maker offering me three new [sic] styles in collars, just recently named: '*Claudine à l'Ecole*' for morning wear; '*Claudine à Paris*' (book-muslin and stitched pleats) and (we must not forget summer and the call of the wilds) '*Claudine s'en va*'.

So thirty years have not thrown into the rag-bag, not yet done away with the little white collar, the round, white, porcelain dish on which dark-haired Polaire's laughing, curly head was served up. It really seems very astonishing to me, and if Mendès came back, he could say that I still did not understand.

M. Willy was very sensitive to misprints and always corrected the proofs of the *Lettres de l'Ouvreuse* with meticulous care. The great number of proper names required scrupulous attention. But at last he had done, at last we left the *Echo* and breathed the black air, the dusty cool of the Rue du Croissant.

"Aren't you dying of thirst?" M. Willy would ask.

Oh! dear yes, I was dying of thirst! Or rather I was thirsting, I was dying for sleep! But instead of going to bed I followed him. Should I know the Brasserie Gambrinus if I saw it again? Did I indeed ever see it except with half-closed, red-lidded eyes? I seem to remember that it was full of beards. I disliked the yellowing stains about the mouths, the hair that had changed colour from constant draughts of beer. One big, goodlooking fellow, Belfort de la Rocque, used to challenge all comers, wagering that he would drink enough to pile up a column of saucers as tall as himself—six foot four. He won, alas! and guffawed loudly in his sheaf of golden beard. He supplemented his beer with absinthe, ate nothing, and remained quite monstrously robust and handsome. And then, suddenly, he died. I have given a passing glimpse of him because he was one of the pillars that upheld, for many nights, a roof of smoke, of Gothic beams, of Louis Quinze mouldings and Renaissance panels above my insecure, useless life.

I always preferred the Latin Quarter to the beer-drinkers' beards and the painted tiles of the 'Pousset'. It was not that my lemonade and red-currant syrup, or my anisette and water tasted any better at the 'Harcourt' or the 'Vachette', but my empty youth, my buried gaiety, called out, although I did not know it, for youth. At the

'Harcourt', sitting beside us at the same table, Pierre Louÿs and André Lebey made us welcome, and Jean de Tinan, on whom M. Willy already had his questing eye.

He was a splendid quarry from every point of view. Consecrated to letters and to death, Jean de Tinan was gentle and delicate in mind and body; his hands were rather frailer than a man's should be, his dark hair curled about a brow that was itself noble and gave nobility to all his features. He could be as affected as a child and at other times so naturally graceful that his charm might have passed for affectation. Neither he nor Pierre Louÿs nor André Lebey were ashamed of being poets. But Jean de Tinan's time was too much taken up by his loves. He liked to please and was kind to the little girls of the 'Harcourt', calling them to our table where Pierre Louÿs gazed at them long and closely with a shortsighted, entomologist's stare. I believe that, in their friendly way, they all three shared the loveliness of a little nineteen-year-old Loute, who was indeed, in her cyclist's cap and breeches, more richly perfect than the most famous beauties. What long blue eyes she had beneath her smooth hair, parted 'à la Cléo de Mérode', and how happy she seemed sitting on Pierre Louÿs' knee, and running her fingers through Jean de Tinan's hair, scented by another woman. I think it is in *Penses-tu réussir?* that Jean de Tinan called me 'Jeannette'. He paid no heed to me, but I much enjoyed looking at him. I said nothing, I listened to the young men's gay, intolerant talk. I was cut off from them; my bad start had set a worse than elderly man between me and every form of youth. Yet I watched with very pleasurable disquiet the movement of Loute's caressing, combing fingers that passed back and forth impartially through the soft, dark curls, or over Pierre Louÿs' stiffly waving mop, I who had never—for

the best of reasons—known the feel of a lover's hair.
André Lebey's head was also crowned with a profusion of
ash-gold locks. That he should be a poet did not surprise
me in the least, but it was the first time I had ever heard
a man discourse at length on furniture and decoration, his
fine hands tracing, as he spoke, harmonious patterns in
the air.

Loute sometimes brought a friend with her, a sombre
young woman, beautiful in her own fashion, who was
fiercely and opaquely silent. Every feature of her beauty
had a brutal, material quality so grossly marked that I
could draw—if I knew how to draw—the jutting curve
of her thick, purple lips, her eyes that were the blue of
angry water, her hair that brooked no contradiction. Was
her name Sylvie, Stella, Sabine? A large, rebellious S is
linked with the image I have kept of her, the picture of a
passer-by, solidly and uselessly engraved on a corner of
my memory. She caught, God knows how, a syphilis of
terrific proportions and died violently in hospital in less
than a week, surrounded by oranges, bunches of violets,
friendly notes signed Pierre Louÿs, Jean de Tinan, Willy,
and even Colette. Her death was an apt finish to her life,
a savage death, enraged and almost dumb. We scarcely
heard her last, harsh, hurried whispers.

Hers is one of the imperishable portraits that chance
has brought together in my memory, that collection of
clear, brightly coloured pictures that gets me nowhere at
all. In this it is almost akin to art, like my handsome
volumes of *Pomology*, or my constellation of glass paper-
weights shaped like jellyfish. Things that are of no use
can be endlessly satisfying.

If the memory of those far off evenings has not yet
been wiped out by time, it is that in my obscurity they
were sweet to me. And perhaps I felt also that a bond

might have, should have existed between one of these young men and myself, some amorous adventure, sensuous and hidden and normal. I liked the presence of their unknown, virile youth and endured the wound of it without complaint. In order not to make a public confession of my deprivation, I created, in *Claudine à Paris*, the character of a little homosexual. So long as I debased them, I could praise the looks of a young male and speak covertly of a secret danger, an unacknowledged attraction. Later, when I made friends with Polaire and saw her in tears over some passing storm—her lover, Pierre L, was twenty-five—heartbroken at a two nights' separation, glorying in the blows given and received, she said to me, her claws still out and her body warm as a rolling cat's: "Oh! Colette! He does smell so lovely, that young brute! And his skin! And his teeth! You just don't know...."

No, I just didn't know.

To speak of the Bohemian life is not to imply a gipsy or roving existence. Our Bohemians seem always to have liked to stay at home, or if they wandered, to wander within very narrow limits. Between 1897 and 1900, drifting from Montparnasse to Montmartre and back again, they scarcely explored Paris. But they sometimes rode bicycles, which is a thing they would not deign to do in 1930. M. Willy hired one for 'country outings'. I used a little racing affair that was painted in blue enamel and had no brake and no mudguards. M. Willy had won it in a raffle held to celebrate the hundredth performance of an operette.[1] Many members of the newspaper world had calves of steel. In the Rue du Croissant, the space under the stairs at *l'Echo* often looked like an old bicycle dump. Only the Marquis de Bièvre, the editor of the obituary column, fulfilled the duties of his office in a donkey-cart, his white rat perched on his shoulder.

Shall I recall the occasional Sunday afternoons, boating on the Marne or on the Seine? It hardly seems worth while; when the time came for them to get to their canoes the oarsmen were sleeping off the effects of wine and a good lunch. Your Sunday sportsmen got up late and ate too much. Slumber descended without distinction of place or person upon all M. Willy's companions, sons of printers or ink-manufacturers, ex-lieutenants of the 31st Regiment of Artillery who had become lawyers

---

[1] The operette *Bouton d'or*.

or solicitors, vague strangers who affected a taste for art and athletics. Maupassant's big muscles and high complexion, his fattish stomach and his liking for after-luncheon wagers, had not yet gone out of fashion.

I would very willingly have been as the others were, sleeping, crimson-faced, in their blue and white jerseys or their shirt-sleeves. But the midday hour saddened me, the vertical light, the scabby grass of the river-banks, the litter of gravel and cigar-ends under the open-air café tables. And so I slipped away by myself to nurse the homesickness that had revived sharply in the shade of the poplars, the scent of the water.

One Sunday we were caught up in an unusually large group and taken off as far as Mantes-la-Jolie. Someone cried: "Why! I know the sub-prefect of this place!" whereupon about sixty wheels, bearing thirty over-sociable cyclists, bowled through the gates of a lovely garden and thrust themselves upon a dark-bearded young official, who, smiling and indefatigable, let them take the fullest, the grossest advantage of his hospitality. The day ended with an improvised concert, given under the trees, at which the High Society of Mantes was able to applaud the passionate singing of Mme Tarquini d'Or. I was twenty-four and had on a pair of zouave trousers, a spotted blouse with balloon sleeves upheld by a framework of stiff muslin, a blue sailor hat. And I thought the young sub-prefect very handsome with his slim figure and his smile and his velvety eye. You will see that I had good taste when I tell you that the name of the sub-prefect of Mantes was Léon Barthou.

I made two friends that day, for I also met and talked with a small, thin young man in a black suit, very dusty from prolonged cycling, whose trousers were elegantly folded round his ankles and held in place with clips. I had seen him going about all day and had noticed his reddened, delicate-looking eyes and melancholy expression. He was sad and slender; later he became square and jovial and bearded, a great epicure, full of self-assurance and good humour. The passing of time has not affected his name, since he had already chosen the pseudonym of Louis Forest.

Winter months, summer months. . . . How long it seemed for June to come round again when I was young! Winter months, drenched with rain and Sunday concerts, while I wilted and grew pale; summer months that restored me to life with the hope that they would last for ever. It was Champagnolle in the Jura, I remember, that saved me for another spell—in 1896? 1897?—from the salamander stove, gloom and resignation. At Champagnolle the inn cost five francs a day.

For five francs we were allowed a room disgraced by a mildewed wall-paper, peeling off and dangling in liana-like strips, by two iron bedsteads and some nasty little curtains fit for wrapping up abortions. But from noon onward the common table was covered with crayfish, quails, hares, partridges, all poached in the neighbourhood. The mountain streams ran between cyclamen and wild strawberries, and my cheeks grew fresh and pink again.

From Champagnolle we went to Lons-le-Saulnier to stay with my husband's family. Before my marriage I had never "lived in someone's house", as I always called it, and it took me a long time to break down the constraint that kept me, not from loving the people who welcomed us, but from yielding to the simple pleasure of letting them see me as I was. Fortunately, the children got the better of me. Three here, four there, not to mention the more distant offshoots of the same stock. They soon found out what I was worth as a maker of flutes, a weaver of grasses, a gatherer of berries. With them I recovered my lost childhood; I told them the names of plants, of stones, lit them a fire using the punt of a bottle as a burning-glass, caught grass-snakes and let them go again, drove the little horse 'Mignon' with proper care and precision, sang the magic formula that bids the snail put out its horns. A chain of quiet, disciplined children closed about me. Were they fond of me? Wherever I went, they followed. I never let them know how beautifully behaved I thought them, how easy of manner, nimble of mind, and how astonished I felt when I considered the difference between their childhood and mine. I, who had been broken in to an outward show of obedience, was as much impressed by the smooth, prompt deference they could always display as by their tidy, well-brushed curls, their clean nails, their smell of English soap, their habit of crooking their little finger when eating a boiled egg. The sound of their voices calling along the paths of the cool little mountain, the name they chose to give me, the pleasure I felt at their taking to me so simply—something of all this comes back when I hear the voice, over the telephone, of Paule, who is a doctor, or her sister, the musician, or their cousin, the interior decorator: "Aunt Colette, tell me, Aunt Colette . . ." The children's company was very sweet to me. My stains and bruises were only superficial, and I was still very young. Perhaps what I needed, without knowing it, was a child born of my own body.

I have known people who were huge: Gaston Leroux is a case in point. M. Willy was not huge, he was bulbous.

The powerful skull, the slightly protuberant eyes, the nose, which was short and had no visible bridge, the drooping cheeks—every one of his features approximated to the curve. His mouth, under the heavy grey-gold moustaches that he dyed for a long while, was narrow, dainty and agreeable-looking, and had something faintly English about its smile. As for his dimpled chin, which was small, weak, you might even say fragile, it seemed the best thing to hide it. Which M. Willy did, at first with a sort of glorified imperial, then with a short beard. It has been said that he bore a marked resemblance to Edward VII. To do justice to a less flattering but no less august truth, I would say that, in fact, the likeness was to Queen Victoria.

Curves and soft surfaces, a baldness that caught the light and held the eye, a modulated voice, a bland outline. Little as I could penetrate these many defensive convexities, I had enough to brood over, darkly. It is indeed a very strange moment, in any life, when fear is born, seeds and takes root, spreads.

The young and healthy-minded do not readily entertain fear. Even a child-victim (people talk of child-victims nowadays, just as they talk of land-surveyors or mothers-in-law, but I use the hyphen with reluctance; it is like the stripe, a symbol of some hideous rank)—even the victimised child is not in terror at every hour of the day; there are always occasions when its tormentors are cheerful and kindly. Perhaps the mouse, between one blow and the next, has respite enough to appreciate the softness of a cat's paw.

Among all the forms of absurd courage, the courage of girls is outstanding. Otherwise there would be fewer marriages and still less of the wild ventures that override everything, even marriage. All that can be said is that if so many girls put their hands into the hairy hand, give their lips to the exasperated convulsion of gluttonous lips and watch without alarm the huge, unknown, male shadow on the wall, it is that the promptings of sexual curiosity are potent in their ears. In a few hours an unscrupulous man will transform an ignorant girl into a prodigy of licentiousness. Disgust will not deter her; disgust has never been a hindrance. Like morality, it comes later. I once wrote: "Dignity is a man's fault." I would have done better to write: "Squeamishness is not a woman's virtue."

A consuming sensual audacity drives too many impatient little beauties into the arms of Lotharios half spoiled by time, and it is with them that, remembering my own youth, I have my quarrel. The seducer does not even have to take trouble; his mettlesome prey is afraid of nothing —at first! In fact she is often surprised: "And is that all? Isn't there anything else people do? At least we can begin again, can't we?" As long as her compliance or her curiosity lasts, she does not see her instructor clearly. Ah! if only she would pay more heed to the shadow on the wall—Priapus! looming huge in the lamplight, the moonlight. The shadow dwindles and is presently revealed as the figure of an already ageing man with blueish eyes, a veiled and impenetrable glance, a terrifying gift for tears, a marvellously husky voice, whose stout body is strangely light and quick, who is hard as an eiderdown stuffed with flints. Such a rich assortment of conflicting subtleties, such a variety of traps!

Protected, absorbed by the kindly children, I spent two or three summers of my youth on the hill of many chalets as peacefully as in a convent sewing-room. I listened to my mother-in-law, my sisters-in-law, my aunts and cousins by marriage, discussing devout Catholic matters.

My head against the back of the basket-chair I let the needlework on which I was clumsily engaged drop on my lap and closed my eyes. The tranquil voices talked on—of the diocese, Lenten fasts, eggless pastries during Passion Week, big fish and little fish, the regrettable tolerance of the bishop who had allowed chocolate to be drunk at the collation: "Made with water of course!" In the scent of ripe plums and *quatre-quarts* cake, I discovered the austerities of a pious family, I heard the jaws of the big scissors chewing the linen.

"When my girls are a little older," Madeleine said, "I will have them taught how to glaze men's shirts."

"Oh! Madeleine," protested Valentine, "surely that's going too far. What do you think, Mother dear?"

The daughterly and ceremonious tone took me back to "Sido"—to "Sido", watching me from afar, reaching out her sensitive antennae, alert and perplexed.

"I think, my child, that it is much too soon to worry your head about such things. Children! Go and look through the telescope! Aren't those our cousins coming up the little path?"

"Yes, Grandmamma! Yes, Grandmamma! And Aunt Martha is with them and so is little Martha! And Louis-Albert too!"

"Well, then, go and tell Fanny we shall need some beer, and extra glasses and more cake-plates. Gabrielle, my child, I believe you're taking a little nap. Some of our relations will be here in a moment."

"Gabrielle", accustomed, now, to her name of 'Colette', would start, apologise, draw the pleats of her blouse down under her belt and straighten the bow of her hair-ribbon—that same hair-ribbon which, in 1935, is knotted round the heads of small girls and young women **and** women who are not so young.

"For once," my mother-in-law would say in her quiet voice, "we shall all be here together."

But, raising her eyes, she would see that her son Albert, her son Henry, were melting away into the distant trees, that her son-in-law had vanished as though by magic, and that 'Gabrielle', on the plea of changing her blouse, had run off, without the least possibility of a return, towards the third of the family chalets, her plait of hair dancing on her legs. . . .

It was on our return from one of these visits to the Franche-Comté that M. Willy decided to tidy his writing-desk. At least I think so, for the memory is linked in my mind with a sense of mourning for a lost, russet September, sweet with bunches of small, sugary grapes and hard, yellow peaches whose hearts were a deep, blood-stained purple. The odious piece of furniture, hideous in its red baize cover and sham ebony paint, was turned out, the whitewood drawers appeared, disgorging a compressed mass of papers, and there came to light the forgotten set of copy-books I had so industriously blackened: *Claudine à l'Ecole*.

"Hullo!" said M. Willy. "I thought I had chucked those away."

He opened one of the copy-books, turned the pages: "It's rather nice."

He opened a second copy-book and said no more. A third, a fourth.

"My God!" he muttered. "I am the bloodiest fool."

He swept up the scattered copy-books just as they were, grabbed his flat-brimmed top hat and bolted to his publisher's. And that is how I became a writer.

At first, I was conscious only of the boredom of having to set to work again under pressing and precise directions.

"Couldn't you add a little spice to these—er—childish affairs?" M. Willy said to me. "A tender and over intimate affection, for instance, between Claudine and one of her friends?" (his actual words were brief and clear). "And dialect, lots of dialect. And rather more playfulness.... D'you see what I mean?"

I saw what he meant, I saw quite well. I also saw, later, that M. Willy was managing to surround my collaboration with something better than mere silence. He got into the habit of making me listen to the lavish compliments that were paid him, of laying his soft hand on my head, of saying: "But you know this child has been most precious to me. Oh! yes, she has! Most precious. She has told me quite delicious things about her board-school."

Young women who write seldom have much sense of moderation (neither have old women, for that matter). And there is nothing that gives more assurance than a mask. The origin and anonymity of 'Claudine' seemed a rather indelicate joke that amused me and that I obediently made broader and broader. I did not read the preface until it was in print; I roared with laughter at the cover: a little girl, disguised as a peasant, sits, an open book upon her knee, writing. On her stockinged feet she wears yellow, comic-opera clogs, Little Red Ridinghood's basket lies beside her, and her curls tumble over her rough, hooded, red cloak.

"What are you laughing at?" M. Willy asked me.

"Why! that picture! And the preface! How can you expect anyone to believe it's true?"

Though I kept my word and remained strictly silent, I found nothing pleasant or natural about the circumstances of this book. Only the companionship of men like Curnonsky, Paul Barlet, Vuillermoz, and their apparent resignation allowed me to get used to it. I could give the names of many others, men who were gay and talented and full of the charming, wasteful good humour of the very young writer who imagines that his gifts and his energies can never be exhausted. Ernest Lajeunesse—as may be seen in a curious series of letters—made difficulties from the first, wanted to be paid, became quarrelsome and finally, after an exchange of threats and abuse, refused, as he puts it: "to sign my work 'Willy' like everyone else." As for Pierre Veber, I shall leave the real author of *Une Passade* to give his own story of a novelist ousted and dispossessed. Jean de Tinan is no longer here to tell us about *Maîtresse d'Esthètes*, and *Un vilain Monsieur*.

To form a habit does not mean to become blinded; I did not think very highly of my first book, or of its three sequels. Time has not changed my opinion, and my judgement on all the *Claudines* is still severe. They frisk and frolic and play the giddy girl altogether too freely. The work reveals, indeed, an irrepressible youthfulness, if only in its lack of technique. But I do not like to rediscover, glancing through these very old books, the suppleness of mood that understood so well what was required of it, the submission to every hint and the already deft manner of avoiding difficulties. To kill off a character, for instance, whom I had come to detest, seems rather grossly casual. And I blame myself when I see how certain things in the *Claudines*—allusions, features that are caricatured yet recognisable, tales that come too near the truth—betray an utter disregard of doing harm. If I am mistaken, all the better! But I am not mistaken.

Claudine à l'Ecole sold well from the start. After a while it sold even better. The series has gone through hundreds of editions and is, I am told, still selling. I only know of it by hearsay. At the time of my first divorce, the copyright already belonged to two publishers who had bought it, out and out, from M. Willy. I had dutifully set my signature beside my husband's on the two contracts. I shall never forgive myself for having done so. The renunciation was indeed the most unpardonable act that fear ever made me commit.

Claudine à Paris and *Claudine s'en va* are the books that displease me most in retrospect. Their chief male character is a mature and attractive man (Renaud), who is hollower, lighter, emptier than the spun-glass balls that hang on Christmas trees and crumble in the hand into a thousand silvery fragments.

In *Claudine à Paris* there appeared for the first time a figure that was henceforth to flourish in all the works of M. Willy—if I may so call them. Henry Maugis is, perhaps, the only disclosure M. Willy has ever made us about himself. And when I say 'us' it is that in my lack of knowledge of this exceptional man I am compelled to speak as a member of the crowd; to have worked for him and beside him taught me to dread, not to know him better. Maugis the woman-fancier, all lit up with fatherly vice, the lover of puns and foreign drinks, the scholarly man, learned in music, letters, Greek, who is fond of duelling, sentimental, unscrupulous, who mocks as he secretly wipes away a tear, who plumps out a bullfinch belly, calls little women in underclothes 'baby', prefers the half-dressed to the naked and socks to silk stockings—that Maugis is no creation of mine.

I think that M. Willy yielded, on the day he invented 'fat Maugis', to one of his chief manias, which was an obsession for self-portraiture, a passion for looking at himself in the glass. From then on, it did not leave him and took a vast quantity of forms that seemed, to the public at large, to be no more than an inordinate sense of self-advertisement. I have my own opinion about this; it may, up to a point, provide an excuse for certain singular lapses, and I give it for what it is worth. I believe that if M. Willy had not suffered from an impediment of the writing faculty, he would never have sought, in order to make his name and his novels known, to overstep the ordinary opportunities of business. Being sterile, he was bound, sooner or later, to go astray. His passion for seeing himself in mirrors became exasperated. Caricatures by Sem and Cappiello, heavier works by Widhopff, sketches by Léandre. On a huge canvas of Pascau's, M. Willy stands high above a seated Colette, and on my face is the same look that can be seen in all the photographs taken of me at that time, a look that is at once submissive, withdrawn, half sweet, half stricken, of which I am a little ashamed.

M. Willy also sat for a large portrait by Jacques-Emile Blanche. The artist destroyed the picture after our two likenesses had more or less vanished of themselves. Blanche had painted us over an old portrait, which he did not like, of Mlle Marie de Heredia in a white dress. Summer passed, and through the new work, which was not yet completed, a young girl appeared, a pale Ophelia, submerged but visible.

I can clearly recall the sinister distortions of the 'Willys' by Leal de Camara. And I remember an *Ouvreuse* over the signature of Rip, a Valloton drawing in dead blacks, like a funeral-announcement, a few Rabiers, fifty sketches by unknown artists, a portrait that had been done very carefully and seriously, signed with some Slav name, and numberless other effigies. The portrait by Boldini records a peak of successful publicity. Who bought it? I don't know. It was flattering, typical and excellent: the cane, the hand, the flat-brimmed top hat tilted a little backwards, the silk-lined coat over the arm, and the highlights picking out the bumps of the clever forehead, the over-luxuriant moustache. As a likeness I found it terrifying, so true to life that my sharpest, most exact dreams have never painted a better, or a worse.

From the heights of Boldini we slide down into a delirious mass of photographs, passing through the multitude of statuettes, models made of cardboard, of india-rubber, silhouettes cut out of wood, frog-like figurines, top hat inkpots—the famous flat-brimmed hat set upside-down to form a container—and other pieces of sculpture, of which one was surely highly significant: at the centre of a marble cross a severed, full-size head of M. Willy rests, and from it spread rays, grouped in clusters like those you see about the heads of saints on barocue altars. I do not remember the name of the craftsman who carved this appalling object. Photographed down, the effulgent head took its place in the series of postcards that M. Willy had printed by the two or three thousand and used in profusion. I have not forgotten a drawing—that appeared, but in what newspapers?—of a flabby-looking Willy, much older and more swollen than life, crowned with a halo.

His note-paper, in all its five or six different sizes, was invariably stamped, in one corner, with the familiar moustachioed head, wearing the stove-pipe hat.

It must be acknowledged that, authorship apart, our fashionable novelist was a most active man, orderly and methodical and with a great power of inspiring others. I still believe that the job of editor on a big daily would have suited him to perfection. He knew how work should be distributed, how to assess exactly the capacities of those about him, how to criticise in a manner that was apt and stimulating, how to judge without praising too highly. These are rare gifts, I feel, that were very ill-employed. Personally, the compliments I got were few and always commonplace. "Delightful, my dear. Yes, yes, I assure you, that will do very well. Since I say so, you can believe me!" His reproofs, on the other hand, written in the margins of my manuscripts (which Paul Barlet preserved; he had been given orders to destroy them) were sharp, brief and to the point: "Not clear." "Too soon." "Had they agreed on this? Well then, say so."

He saw to everything, neglected no opportunity; for a while he never allowed a topical Revue to appear at the end of the year without its caustic scene on Willy and Claudine. He would arrange and talk over the sketches himself with the authors of the Revue.

The immense size of his correspondence was always disconcerting—that is his own contribution to it; no one was ever entrusted with that formidable task. He never filed a letter without adding, in his own hand, in the top left-hand corner: "Answered on the ——" When *Claudine* became well-known, things got even worse. Letters, portraits of under-age maidens in socks and white collars dripped from every pocket of the 'Father of Claudine', as he liked to be called. The pernicious adolescents themselves flowed in at the very doors of a dwelling that I really can no longer refer to as conjugal.

A little more and there would have been nowhere for me to put my blotting-pad and laid paper copybooks, if, now that the money was coming in, we had not moved. The Rue de Courcelles gave us sunny accommodation, first at No. 93 and then at 177 *bis*.

My husband, by this time, had been able to estimate the value of my output, and it was he, as soon as we settled in our third flat, who saw to it that I had a good table, a lamp with a green globe, the comfort befitting a scribe. To reach my narrow domain I had to go through the drawing-room, which was a sort of stylised tavern, furnished with tables and benches of polished wood. One day I found M. Willy there in close proximity to an unknown lady. With the ease that comes from long habit, with the free humour (which I was acquiring) of the indispensable employee, I paused a moment as I went by and whispered urgently in M. Willy's ear: "Hurry up! For God's sake, hurry up! The next one has been waiting for a quarter of an hour!" After all, what had I to lose? A year before, a joke of this kind would have cost me—yes, quite a lot! But on this occasion, if you please, M. Willy was flattered.

So there was no longer any need to protect or to shift a sphere of solitude that did not go beyond the edges of the table, the circle of light shed by the lamp, the dull green walls of my little drawing-room-jail. Pens, 'Flamant No. 2' nibs, ruled laid paper, scented glue, long, stork-shaped German scissors, unnecessary coloured pencils, childish implements of a rather finicking worker. Since I could not like my life, I liked its setting, and every afternoon I sat and wrote with an indolent air while M. Willy's business activities took him out and about in a hired brougham. At that time a hired carriage and two horses a day cost less than six hundred francs a month, for Comoy, the livery-man, let us have them at specially reduced, 'professional' prices. I and my dog used to go out on foot before lunch, thus avoiding the eccentricities of the morning horse, which was black, emphatic, superb to look upon, but somewhat difficult to manage, being ungelded and given, at every season of the year, to emitting cries of a sudden and savage nature.

Affluence! Luxury! I was dazzled by the grant of a three hundred francs a month bonus—except in the summer months, which did not count. Three hundred francs, if you please, for me to spend as I liked, three hundred francs that had nothing to do with the famous 'Book'. What a lot you could buy, in those days, for three hundred francs! It was my turn, now, to give "Sido" presents. She chose them herself, sticks of pure cocoa from Hédiard, a quilted bed-jacket, fine wool stockings, books. But my supreme gift to her was a lie: my pretence of happiness. Hour by hour I fought my unutterable yearning to go back to her, to be with her, torn and bleeding, unknown and penniless, a burden on the last days of her life. And when I think of the person I was during those long years of stubborn self-control, of filial deceit, come, come, I don't believe I am as bad as all that.

CLAUDINE S'EN VA gave me a lot of trouble. In the first place there was the Bayreuth atmosphere that I had to go and find in Bayreuth itself. This might have been considered a pleasure-trip, since I went at the expense of the *Echo de Paris* with the *Ouvreuse du Cirque d'été*, but I had no liking for the celebrated place of pilgrimage and the custom that obliged the pilgrim to lodge with the inhabitants. A coffin-like bed and sheets that buttoned on to the blankets, "*Gute Nacht!*" from Frau Mader in curl-papers, from Herr Mader in shirt-sleeves and braces, the nocturnal labours of a baker just under the floor—so much for the nights. By day I can set down on the credit side the three or four hours of music, piously absorbed in the 'gasometer', and the delight of some incomparable German voices. Between the performance and the time we went to bed, and again between the time we got up and lunch, came the brief, agitated hour, the anxious hour when M. Willy waited for his helpers, the providers of notes and material for his musical articles: "Quick, my dear, quick! It's eleven and you said you'd be here at ten. You're wearing my nerves to a frazzle."

What has become of the stock-in-trade of the Wagnerian bazaar, the inexhaustible supply of Grails and hanaps, the ridged balls of turned wood that reproduced in profile the famous nut-cracker features; the papers, paper-weights, jewellery, leather-work? The Franconian heat poured down, covering the angel-robes of the fanatics with fine, sooty dust.

"Take plenty of notes," M. Willy advised me. "They're always useful. I have no memory."

Failing the positive energy that would have saved me from my craven state, I applied the force of inertia and took no notes. With the result that the ceremonies of the Wagner worship remain as floating, misty and uncertain as I was myself, rocking vaguely here and there in the old two-horse carriages, drawn by one horse, between Mendès, voluble and full of beer, blond and rufous like Siegfried, Dr. Pozzi in his white clothes, black-bearded as a sultan, soft-eyed as a houri, massive foreign ladies with heavy ropes of golden hair, and Wagner junior, small of body, large of head, low of rump and alarmingly ubiquitous.

Back in Paris, I set to work with the slow, plodding, clerk-like determination that has never left me.

"If you want my help for Maugis," said M. Willy, "leave gaps."

I left no gaps. A challenge has provided entertainment for many an anonymous toiler, many a captive. My 'in the manner of ——' held together perfectly, my Maugis talked pure, original Maugis.

"Bravo!" said M. Willy coldly.

But I did not always get immediate and spontaneous applause. A few pages that were rather too poetical—there is no use looking for them, they no longer exist—brought my manuscript back to me, flung across the table with the acid comment of my reader-critic: "I did not know I had married the last of the lyric poets."

Hard words, but true, no doubt, and they were not wasted on me.

The second act of *Claudine à Paris* is set in a restaurant called the 'Convalescent Mouse'. In the middle of the act, at the moment when tradition demands the appearance of a star, whether the said star is a trick bed or a naked woman or an acrobatic dancer, a character makes his entrance from the back of the stage, pauses, speaks a few lines, while the other actors, the people who are drinking or supping, the waiters and *maîtres d'hotel*, look on, watching him with an air of recognition, of mingled curiosity and irony and respect: "Maugis. . . . Why! it's Maugis! What will you have, Monsieur Maugis?", etc., etc.

Everything was there, the hat, the cane, the moustaches, the imperial: Maugis of the 'Bouffes' was a complete double of M. Willy. A clever make-up heightened the likeness and increased my discomfort, which was all the greater in that the character was purely episodic, unnecessary, had no bearing on the plot, merely said his half-dozen insignificant lines and vanished into the wings from which he should never have emerged. The trouble was that he did emerge, every evening. Every evening M. Willy's double came to life, talked, copied the familiar gestures, the offhand manner, the way of holding the head, challenged or was challenged to a duel which he fought, wounding his opponent, during the second interval, so as to survive in the audience's mind beyond the close of the second act. Even if I did not actually see him, I knew the precise moment when the double would begin to speak and move, wearing the flat-brimmed top hat provided by the author's munificence and his love for correct detail. Worse than that, in ordering his sauerkraut and his beer, the double used the artificial form of speech that blossoms in the writings of Félix Fénéon, mars the work of Huysmans, often makes Verlaine's letters pretentious and belongs, in truth, to no one, not even to Alcanter de Brahm:

"*Kellner!*" cried Maugis. "May there, by your courtesy, be set before me sauerkraut and sausages, begetters of pyrosis, and a draught of that sickly but salicylated dish-water that is, in your impudence, ycelpt Munich beer. O Beer of Munich! Liquid velvet! Forgive them, they know not what they drink."

I believe that prose of this type, devoid of simplicity and even of clarity, phrases full of twists and arabesques, interplay of syllables, indirect allusions, garnished with technical terms and puns, making a show of etymological erudition, toying with 'olde' French, with slang, with foreign languages living or dead—I am convinced that such prose, by betraying a thirst to startle and astonish, betrays the character of the man who uses it. If you wanted to discover the true secret of its mannerisms, would you not have to go back a very long way, to a boy's timidity, the weaknesses and affectations of a beginner and a profound self-doubt?

With the appearance of the Maugis-double on the stage, M. Willy's intoxication reached the acute, delirious phase. Surrounded by the evidence of an ever-increasing success, he began to reverence, as well as to exploit, his own symbols. From the moment your negro sorcerer starts to believe in the virtues of the noxious remedy he is concocting, you must fear for the sorcerer rather than for his patient. But perhaps I should put down to natural instability the excitement that robbed M. Willy of much of his caution, disclosed his craze for notoriety, any kind of notoriety, and that was at the root, maybe, of the feverish anxiety, the haste, "Quick, dear, quick!" neither of which have ever been explained.

But since my sorcerer continued, in private life, to be exactly like himself—and I do not feel called upon to comment upon the subject—I had quite enough to do dealing with my own ever present fears. You do not notice changes in what is always before you. Haunted by money to a perilous degree, imprudent and darkly secretive, weakly and plaintive when it served him, disarming when he chose, he never failed to provide me, throughout the years that I made prosperous, with my share of confused pleasure and clearly defined pain. Under this régime I acquired, I developed and shaped within me, the ways and temper of a china-repairer. A prison is indeed one of the best workshops. I know what I am talking about: a real prison, the sound of the key turning in the lock and four hours claustration before I was free again. "Show your credentials!" What I had to show were so many well-filled pages. I am aware that these details of a routine jailing do me little honour, and I do not enjoy looking like a shorn sheep. But their somewhat Gothic flavour and the respect due to freakish truths give them their place here. The window, after all, was not barred, and I had only to break my halter. And so—peace be upon the hand, now dead, that did not hesitate to turn the key! It taught me my most essential art, which is not that of writing but the domestic art of knowing how to wait, to conceal, to save up crumbs, to reglue, regild, change the worst into the not-so-bad, how to lose and recover in the same moment that frivolous thing, a taste for life. What I chiefly learnt was how to enjoy, between four walls, almost every secret flight, and also to compromise, to bargain and finally, when the "Quick! My God! Quick!" fell upon me, to hint, "Perhaps I could work faster in the country."

If the 'case against M. Willy' were only that of an ordinary man who engaged other men to write the books he signed, it would not deserve very much attention. There will always, alas! be too many starving folk in our profession for the job of 'ghost' to become extinct. The case of M. Willy had one unique and remarkable feature: the man who did not write was more talented than the men who wrote in his stead. I do not propose to repeat their names or to try to make out what is due to Maurice, to Paul, to Eugène, to Jean, to Raymond, and many others. To do so, I would need to have known them all.

M. Willy was well-informed on every subject; he had a lively, caustic wit and could 'talk' a short article for one of the lighter weeklies, an imaginative sketch (that left little to the imagination) infinitely better than it was ever in fact transcribed by the furtive young man who brought him his 'copy' in regular instalments, six sheets at a time. If he had written a novel it would have been probably more ingenious, most certainly in better taste, than the books whose titles I am omitting. But he never wrote a novel. It is a pity. Between the wish, the need to produce saleable printed matter, and the act of writing, this strange author encountered an obstacle that I have never been able to picture—some barrier of a peculiar shape and quality, unknown, possibly terrifying. His letters express only the *refusal* to write. A tiny article, a few lines long, gives rise to ten pages of feverish correspondence, five or six letters, addressed to the usual practitioner, of detailed instructions, urgent demands, anxious enquiries. Or to eager express-cards and telegrams:

"*Do me some gossip-column stories in dialogue, as short as possible, fifteen lines, on cheap seaside resort. Characters: Marcel Ballot, Marquis of Chasseloup-Laubat, Frank Richardson, famous English essayist, Willy in company of sumptuous Englishwomen in skin-tight bathing-dresses. One of said bathing-dresses splits and sets the kodaks clicking. Two rival casinos, anaemic baccarat, bancos at two louis. Important: 'Her husband bolted with a girl called Maud. She bolted after them.' Well done! 'That's a true Marriage à la Maud' (or: that follows the Maud).*"

This set of precise directions, which is as long if not longer than the required paragraph, will give the curious enquirer some light upon an undeniable condition of morbid laziness and perhaps on that *timidity* of expression I referred to earlier.

"*Your Maugis Amoureux is very, very good. When do you expect to finish it!*" You would imagine, reading little notes of this kind, that they were inspired by nothing warmer than a friendly, half-indifferent politeness. "*Look here, old chap—something that might be rather choice to do. Something on the lines of dear old* Quo Vadis *or everybody's* Aphrodite. *Greek bilge or Roman b . . . s? That will depend on the material I can get hold of. Am rummaging round Germany to see if there is anything we could remanipulate with elegance and delicacy. . . . Some of the Herondas Dialogues might be useful, or that diarrhoea of Greek tales, Heliodorus, Achilles Tatius, all exactly the same, all equally stupid.*"

Was anything—any form of travel, of research, of compilation—was *everything*, then, better than a few hours, a few days' concentration, alone with a blank sheet of paper? It is all very mysterious and sad.

For the big Sunday concerts a corps of despatch-riders was mobilised, carefully picked men who galloped from Colonne to Pasdeloup, from Pasdeloup to the Conservatoire, exchanged stalls, snatched a seat from beneath the confederate who had been mounting guard: *"Dear Sir. Tomorrow, at the Risler concert, you are requested to advance swiftly upon stall No. 26, which will be occupied by the backside of a gentleman in black—black, black as my soul. This sombre individual (Aussaresses by name) will deliver up to you some notes (what did you think?) on the concert if you stand him a beer . . ."* etc., etc.

Marches and countermarches, passwords, plots, conferences at G.H.Q., the final fitting together of the jigsaw—what a lot of trouble! Surely it would have been easier for a man who had an excellent ear, who could accompany himself on the piano and sing in a small, pleasantly veiled tenor voice—surely such a man should have found it easier to write? No. Everything was easy to him, everything was lawful, except the task of writing.

As for the novels, it took me a long time to understand the system of interchange and substitution that was applied to them and that worked safely enough until the inventor of the system himself brought it to grief. No harm can come to anyone if I explain its intricacies now. The people who fancy that they see in what I am saying a bitter spirit, a rancid and venomous passion, are quite mistaken. In a woman who has been compelled to rise more than once from her ashes, or merely to struggle out, unaided, from the mass of bricks, mortar, planks and plaster that had fallen on her head, there cannot be, after over thirty years, passion or venom, but only pity of a cold sort and laughter that is not at all kindly, I must admit, and is directed at herself as much as at the chief character of her story. Moreover, I find M. Willy vastly more interesting than the bunch of heroes—royal bastards, secret favourites, magicians and magi—who gravitate uncomfortably round the lesser figures of history and who are constantly being plucked out of their dim circuits by hands that are more forceful than discreet, and dragged, blinking and bedizened, into the limelight. I consider that my hero, my highwayman of the lesser paths of literary history, is of a class and a stature to excite and repay curiosity.

Where did he get the first idea for a novel, the first, bare outline of a plot? No matter. In its original shape the Idea did not stay with him for more than a moment. Off it went instantly, accompanied by a handwritten letter, to the cleverest specialist, the dear, jolly fellow who had not yet become the Prince of Gastronomes but was already skin-full of wit and fun and finesse: *"Cur, old man, what about it? The enclosed fancy has just sprouted in my brain, a frail thing yet dainty withal. . . . Cast your expert eye upon this grub and map out, in fifty pages, its future destiny. Or crush it, yet unborn, beneath your noble feet."*

On its return, the Idea would be cleansed of its new form and the traces of an alien hand and would reappear type-written, in a fresh envelope—and with a fresh address: *"Petipol, my dear chap! Help! Help! Here is my lastborn infant. Can you, in a month, get the substance of a light novel out of it? Setting: a small, northern, seaside resort, damp bathing-dresses, casino, ten-penny Boule, Maugis gone there to invigorate his de-iodized constitution, a little girl with lusty legs . . . etc."*

The occult Petipol having duly crystallised the necessary 'substances', the manuscript, retyped, would assume yet another virgin wrapper and depart, bearing a letter, to a third therapeutist: *"No, my dear friend, no, things are not going well. A state of extraordinary prostration, extraordinarily unwarranted, agonising headaches, and those blanks in the mind that fill me with anguish. God! the nights, the endless, empty hours! You ask how my latest book is going! Here it is. Isn't it enough to make one bash one's head against the wall? You alone with your skill and charm, your delicacy of expression, your happy choice of phrase—your gifts in fact, which I respect too deeply for jealousy—only you can transfuse into this pauper's child the rich and healthy blood that . . .", etc., etc. "Needless to say, a fitting remuneration will . . .", etc.*

It sometimes happened, in spite of the combination of doctors and treatments, that the work had to go the rounds of the honourable company a second time, clad, after each visit, in its cowl and cloak of clean typing.

This brief record can convey no more than a faint notion of the cares and anxieties of the final signatory, the constant vigilance required to navigate seas obstructed, not by reefs or sandbanks, but by havens of salvation. Who could guess even at the number of letter-cards sent, of personal calls paid and flights of stairs climbed? M. Willy's microscopic handwriting with its rising lines and lanceolated word-endings—as you see, I have not forgotten that I once studied graphology—shows that he had taste of the highest order, a strong critical sense, the faculty of rapid recovery, the wish to please and a power of dissimulation so remarkable that the script, which is small at the start of a letter, becomes gradually, and without any graphic change, too tiny to be read even with a magnifying glass, like those feats of penmanship that give you—if you can decipher them!—the entire *Creed* on the back of a postage stamp.

I have often thought that M. Willy suffered from a sort of agoraphobia, that he had a nervous horror of the blank page. His correspondence shows a preference for postcards, letter-cards, half- or quarter-sheets of note-paper, the flaps of envelopes, triangles cut off and used just as they are, even newspaper wrappers. And again, on these scraps, the writing is huddled in the far corners. Sometimes he scribbles the answers in the margins of the letters he has received and so posts them back.

I fancy he was frequently overcome by fits of weakness, a pathological shrinking, when he considered the courage, the grim fortitude that is needed to sit without disgust before the virgin field, the naked page, unscored by arabesques, headings, scratched-out words, the cold, indifferent paper, white and blinding, thankless, greedy. Or perhaps work bored him so intolerably—which can happen, does happen; boredom can kill—that he preferred to exchange the anguish of it for the perils and problems of the managerial chair, among which, alas! the question of quality was the least important.

Perhaps he enjoyed his acid, pedagogic prestige, the biting comments he used to let fall, drily, from the heights of his superiority, on to my bent head, or that he wrote in the margins of my manuscripts. Nothing will rid me of the conviction that he was a born critic, although even the opinions on which he based his judgements were borrowed from other people—a born monitor, incisive, quick to find the sensitive spot, to give the faintly cruel thrust that reawakens a drowsy self-esteem.

He must, in the old days, have often believed that he was on the point of writing, that he was about to write, that he was, in fact, writing. And then, as he felt the pen within his fingers, there would come a slackening, a collapse of the will, and his illusion vanished:

"*Your* Maugis Amoureux *is very very good. I like the tone of it immensely. A good dodge: Maugis, disappointed in his yearnings for sweet innocence, chucks loathly Bayreuth and hasting back to Paris recounts how* passus est. *Hence, some moderation in the Bayreuth passages. Leave gaps.*

"*All the same, as I shall have very little time, don't leave too much space for Bayreuth, just enough to rag the music and the town.*

"*P.S. On second thoughts, no, don't leave any gaps. I'll insert a word or two here and there in your stuff—up to ten lines in all. At most . . .*"

Between the first and the third paragraph, between the words: "*Leave gaps!*" and the words: "*On second thoughts, no, don't leave any gaps*", a tragedy has taken place, a struggle, a sudden stiffening of pride, followed by what Balzac calls in old French, in his *Contes Drolatiques*, a '*déflocquement*', the ghastly state of prostration that seems to turn the very bones to water, to unknit the fibres of the will. Was his a case of that paralysis, that complete inability to act, which some drug-takers experience when faced with an effort? I believe not. M. Willy was addicted to remedies but not, to my knowledge, to poison. One of his letters refers to opium and P-J. Toulet with a certain naïvety. He appears to confuse the morphinomaniac with the opium-smoker, and describes Toulet as the simultaneous victim of the 'dark vapour' and excessive drink.

But these are all conjectures and oddities for which I have never found an explanation. Nor shall I ever know the reason for his chronic haste: "As I shall have very little time . . . Quick, my dear, quick! . . . Run along now, old chap . . . Need I remind you, my dear Colette, of the extreme urgency . . ." Sufferers from a creeping illness who know their days are counted, may say aloud: "I am in a hurry." Under their breath, they whisper: "I am pursued. . . ." M. Willy, although somewhat the worse for wear, was a strong man; he died at seventy-five. He probably endured no such tortures, so that his impatience was no more than a mental trick—'trick' being, perhaps, a pet name for 'neurosis'.

When the time had come for me to stop dead, like a horse shying—the word 'shying' conveys, I think, the best picture of the sudden jerk, the complete, stubborn refusal—I received a letter from M. Willy. It reached me in the little flat to which I had retreated with my cat, my bulldog, my shipwrecked books, and coming on top of a prodigious din of threats, rattling weapons, thunder and lightning, it astonished me greatly. In the precise tones to which I had so long been accustomed, my husband asked me to write, for his next novel, twenty pages of landscape, "as you know so well how to write them", and offered me—a thousand francs! A thousand francs of before the war, a thousand francs on top of a divorce, a thousand francs for twenty pages when, for the four volumes of *Claudine* . . . I felt I was dreaming. The dream materialised next day in the shape of a typewritten script. But—the story was set in the Principality of Monaco, which I hardly knew and did not like, so I returned it, pleading incompetence. M. Willy telegraphed: "If novel situated Franche Comté, would you accept? If so, action emigrates East."

Also by telegram and in similarly concise terms, I agreed. It will presently be seen why I preferred to recall and to paint the Franche Comté scene.

What followed gave rise to rather an amusing incident that was described to me later by the good fellow who did the odd jobs at M. Willy's, saw to the post, made up the parcels of typewritten copies, carried them here and there. Overwhelmed with orders and injunctions, cursed on principle as a measure of precaution, slanged in a friendly way up hill and down dale, laden with racing tips and three or four confidential notes for the 'curly-headed baby', the 'adorable kid', the 'child-princess', and other conquests of tender years, poor X—— sweated freely, winter and summer.

After I had made my few pages of contribution to the Besançon-ex-Monaco novel and had returned it, M. Willy ran through the new passages and tossed the completed manuscript to X——.

"Take it to the printers. At the double. And tell them to let me have the galleys quick, my God, quick!"

In its proof-form, the novel came flying back, swift as a boomerang, into its master's hands.

"Get on with it, X——. Hurry up and do your corrections so that I can pass it for the press. There's no time to wait for a second set of proofs."

The perspiring X—— obeyed. Having finished his correcting, he did as he was accustomed to do and reclothed the object in its clean wrapper. As he knotted the pink tape, he glanced at his master's bent and harassed back and chanced a timid enquiry:

"Is it true you can see the sea from Besançon?"

Getting no answer beyond an irritable shrug of the broad shoulders, X—— did not insist.

"I'm off now, Guv'nor," he murmured.

M. Willy woke suddenly from his trance of concentration.

"What's that? What was it you asked me just now?"

"Oh!" cried X——, flushing scarlet. "It's nothing—it's not worth bothering—I was only thinking. . . . It seemed funny that you should see the sea from Besançon."

M. Willy, smiling—the kindly despot—upon his minion, let fall a string of harmless insults. He certainly did not expect X—— to bristle up.

"But see here, Guv'nor, honestly! I didn't invent, that

from Besançon . . . It's at the beginning of your new novel: '*Leaning on the balcony-rail of his smart little Besançon villa, Monsieur Tardot was amusing himself spitting into the Vasty Deep.*' That's a proof, isn't it, that I'm not lying?"

With the agility peculiar to fat men, with the silent, melting ease that I have seen in no one else (I might add that he was an exquisite dancer), M. Willy rose from his chair:

"Undo that parcel," he said. "There are one or two little mistakes I must have *another* look at."

Sitting down to his desk and his corrections, he talked and chuckled to himself:

"The way things happen! It's too comic. You could make a story out of it. I do believe I'll make a story out of it some day."

At the faintest stir of memory, the little estate of 'Monts-Boucons' comes back to me. I see its roof of almost black tiles, its Directoire façade—that was probably no older than Charles X—painted in a yellowish monochrome, its copses, its arch of broken rocks in the best Hubert Robert manner. M. Willy appeared to give the place to me, the house and the little farm and the ten or twelve acres of land: "All this is yours." Three years later he took them away again: "Nothing of this is yours any longer, or mine."

The orchard was very old; it still yielded a meagre crop of delicious fruit. Up there, from June till November, for three or four years running, I led a life as lonely as a shepherd's. Needless to say, M. Willy kept a watchful eye upon my loneliness and came to visit it himself from time to time. He used to arrive dead beat and go off overwhelmed, cursing the weight of his "labours" and the necessity of being "tied to Paris" in the middle of summer. He would leave behind him in my care ("These repulsive volumes are worth a very great deal of money") a number of small trunks full of obscene literature, English as well as French, some of it ancient; and then proceed to remove them.

My more acute distress went with him, and yet his sudden going still hurt something in me, the persistent normal dream: a couple living together in the country. But, away from his presence, I felt myself becoming once again a better person, that is to say better fitted to live upon my own resources and as punctual and orderly as though I already knew that discipline is the cure for every ill.

At six o'clock in the summer, at seven in autumn, I was out of doors, aware of the rain-drenched roses, or the red leaves of the cherry-trees quivering in the red November dawn. The silver-coated rats squatted at ease, eating their meal of grapes straight from the vine; the big snake, caught in the trellis of the hen-run, could not escape the fowls' ferocity. The swallows ruled the cat with extreme rigour, driving it away with sharp blows of their beaks and shrill whistling war-cries from the barn and the rows of nests that lined every rafter. I had a bulldog, 'Toby-Dog', who lived in a turmoil or a swoon of emotion, and a long, luxurious, subtle angora cat, "Kiki-the-Demure'.

A *pégot* cat—the *pégot* cats of the Franche-Comté are those that follow like dogs—attached herself to me. Fond, familiar beasts, infinitely precious. I did not talk to them a great deal since they were always with me. Another came to join our company, an elderly half-bred horse, slim-legged and light-footed, torn by a thousand lashes, covered with wounds, that I bought and cared for as best I could and presently rode. We were an odd sight, the two of us, he in his dressings, with pads of greased linen between his skin and the saddle-girths, and bandages of soft rag about his fetlocks, I astride him in checked bicycle bloomers of the zouave type. To be on the safe side, I went to the military riding-school at Saint-Claude and called upon the excellent help and advice of Calame, the riding-master; for a week or so I went round and round, over the fences, at the tail of the last horse, behind four would-be pupils of the Saint-Maizant academy. "Tuck in your buttocks! Tuck in your buttocks!" Calame shouted at me in his flat, Franche-Comté voice. "'Pon my word! You do me more credit than all these bumpkins!"

I also bought, for two or three hundred francs, during the last year, a charming relic, an old *petit-duc* and its silver-buckled harness. The *petit-duc* is a carriage that is something between a fairy chariot and a child's push-cart. There is room for two people, but no coachman's box, and the body is set so low that your feet are almost level with the road. Without stopping or disturbing anybody, you can step out and gather hedge roses and mushrooms, scabious, oak-apples, wild strawberries, and, when you please, step in again. The horse saunters, browses, dreams beside you. I used to fill the empty seat with flowers and fruit and chestnuts. One day I brought back my most splendid find, bottles of wine—Volnay, Chambertin, Corton, and a forty-year-old Frontignan, glowing with warmth and amber sunshine. They were all wines of a respectable age and vintage, that I had picked up for a few francs at a wayside tavern that was changing hands.

Though many years have passed, the savour of those Franche-Comté days is still alive in me, nothing has been lost of the myriad sights and scents, the long hours of work and study, the sadness. I was, in fact, learning to live. Can you learn to live? Yes, if you are not happy. There is no virtue in felicity. To endure without happiness and not to droop, not to pine, is a pursuit in itself, you might almost say a profession. I was writing *La Retraite Sentimentale* at the time, a book that tells of the light adventures of a young woman, Annie by name, who likes men very much, and of Marcel, who does not like women at all. As I wrote, a new strength was growing in me that had no connection with literature. But it gave way if I tried it too hard; I had not yet reached the point of wishing to leave the 'domestic hearth', and the work that was even more domestic than the hearth. But I was changing. Slowly, if you like, but what matter? To change is the great thing.

I had become vaguely aware of a duty towards myself, which was to write something other than the *Claudines*. And so, drop by drop, I squeezed out the *Dialogues des Bêtes*. In it I enjoyed the moderate but honourable satisfaction of not talking about love. I had a further reward, the best of all: Francis Jammes' fine preface. All my novels, after that, dwelt most persistently upon love, and I have not grown tired of the subject. But I brought it back into my books and found pleasure in it when I had recovered my respect for love—and for myself.

It is the image in the mind that binds us to our lost treasures, but it is the loss that shapes the image, gathers the flowers, weaves the garland. What would I have kept of the Monts-Boucons if M. Willy had not taken them from me? Less, perhaps, than I have now. I cried out, as we all cry out, losing a passion that is in its first sweetness: "How can I live without the Monts-Boucons?" And. . . . And I laid to my breast, and later hung up before me, the garland of yellow leaves, intermingled with cherries half-honeyed by the fierce Franche-Comté summers, with clusters of sleepy wasps, dug at dawn, basketful by basketful, from their potent subterranean nests. And the handful of speckled feathers, quills of my five goshawks that pursued the snakes and lizards so vigorously, that perched so insolently upon the smallest wild quince tree. They would let me draw quite close to them, staring at me as I stared into their eyes, and then would rise into the air in a spreading wheel of wings. That is my memory of the Monts-Boucons. Before that, nothing had been of real account but my own native

Puisaye. My Puisaye garland is of flowering rushes, the great rose-coloured butoma blossoms rising from the lake, bolt upright upon their own reflections in the water, and the berry of the rowan and the sorb-apple of the service-tree, and the medlar, ruddy and tough, that will not ripen in the summer sun but softens and yields to autumn. It is the water-caltrops with its four sharp horns, its greyish flesh that tastes of tench and lentils; it is the red, the white, the purple heather, growing in a soil as light as birch ashes. It is the bulrush with its brown rat's fur and, to bind my wreath together, the snake that swims across the pool, its little chin just ruffling the water. Nothing, no hand, no storm, can take from me the marshes of my childhood, the fruitful, swampy places by the ponds, where the reeds grow. Every year the harvest of rushes is cut down and roughly plaited into mats, but it is never altogether dry before the plaiting. My bedroom had no other comfort than these rush-carpets, spread over the cold red tiles, and no other scent. Green scent of earth and water, marsh fever that we brought into our homes like some gentle beast, wild and sweet of breath— it is with me still, I press it close, between my pillow and my cheek, and it breathes as I breathe.

WHAT Polaire made of 'Claudine' is quite unforgettable. Even where she went wrong, where she refused to obey the authors' and the producer's directions, to her audience she was invariably right and she never made a slip that was not happy. She asked for the part, claimed it for herself, with the inspired tenacity of a visionary: "No, Monsieur Vili, Claudine is not So-and-So; nor Mrs. Thingummy, nor Miss This-and-That or Whatnot. . . . No, Monsieur Vili, *I* am Claudine."

She was living, when I first knew her, in a snug little house that followed the usual pattern of snug little houses—a cosy, pleasant place. Like everyone else, I had seen her in the songs and dances that had made her famous. Mme Landolf used to enjoy inventing amazing dresses for her. A paper-doll's dress in little loose frills of changing blue and green taffetas; a dress the colour of Polaire's skin with a Prairie Indian's diadem of purple feathers; a mulatto's dress of purest white, all froth and snow; a dress that hid a rainbow under its skirt and spread it wide about the slim, black, silky legs and their exotic strength and agility and elegance. I had applauded Polaire in her epileptic frenzy at the chorus of *Hildebrand*:

> *Hildebrand, Hildebrand,*
> *Your name is thrilling, it's so grand!*

and in the unexpected and absurd little song with words —most surprisingly!—by Paul Leclerc:

I love all beasts and can't say which
I fancy most, the cat, the monkey
The frog, the camel or the donkey.
I'd even cuddle an old bitch
But perhaps my greatest pet
Is my little marmoset. . . .

Watching her, admiring the harmony between the long line of the eyes and the long line of the mouth, I had borne with the dubious allusions of the 'Portrait of a little Cat':

Il est tout petit, frais et rond,
Tout velouté comme une pêche . . .

I will quote the end of the song, which was affected and shocking, indelicate and without candour, like the the devices that sometimes appeared on match-boxes in those days:

Allons, mon p'tit matou,
Viens vite, dis-moi tout,
Pas possible? . . . *Vraiment!*
Parole? . . . *Ah! c'est charmant!*

(to the audience)

Si vous voulez surprendre
C' que sa pudeur cacha
Faudrait, pour mieux m' comprendre,
Donner vot' langue au chat!

A poor thing. Polaire sang it screwing up her body and quivering like a wasp in a jam-pot; her lips smiled convulsively as though she had been sucking a sour lemon.

I had also seen her come on to the stage with her skipping-rope, skipping as fast as she was able: "Mustard! Pepper!" One evening she caught her foot in the rope and fell with a shriek: "*Oh! merde!*" Springing up again in a single, wild leap, she crept towards the footlights, an appalled and terrified child, her hands clapped over her mouth. Guiltily she stammered, stressing her e-sounds as she still does: "Messieu-eurs, Mesdames—I beg your pardon. I couldn't help it. I can only hope you will forgive me. . . ."

But I had never seen her outside the theatre. I went to call on her with M. Willy. She was alone; under her arm she carried a tiny, silky-coated black and tan toy-terrier, whose name I was never able to get clear. "She's my Gaguille," Polaire would say, or: "Where are you, my Lelette?" Or again: "I went for a walk to please Troutrouille," or: "The Lilac Duckling is still constipated."

On the day of our first meeting Polaire was dressed like a well brought up young girl in navy blue or dark green. She was letting her famous short hair—which was not black but a natural shade of chestnut—grow longer and had tied it with a ribbon on the nape of her neck. She was not heavily made up. Except for the bistre shadow on her lids, the mascara of her wonderful long lashes, a faintly purple rouge on her lips, she glowed with her own radiance that flashed and faded, flashed again, a shining that seemed near to tears in her eyes' sad infinity, a long-drawn, unhappy smile, all the pathetic appeals that contradicted her diabolic eyebrows, her dancing ankles, restless as a mountain goat's, the sudden jerks and snake-twists of her tiny waist, and that proclaimed, luminous and moist and tender, that the soul of Polaire had got into the wrong body.

Some of the symptoms of this singular error were considered highly comical, her nervous trick, for instance, of jigging her body, of skipping up and down as though the ground burnt her busy, nimble feet. She did it at the rehearsals of *Claudine à Paris*, hopping from one foot to the other in her white convolvulus dress, so that M. Willy presently reproved her: "For God's sake, Polaire! Can't you keep still! You look like a flower that wants to do weewee!"

Polaire, horrified, flushed from pale to darkest amber: "Oh Vili! How could you use such a word! You should call it 'going to the back garden'."

In the theatre her approach to her art was unusual. She understood all the more delicate shades, the subtleties, the thoughts that were suggested, half concealed, and expressed them to perfection; but with the grossly obvious she became awkward, and humour often made her sad. But when did Polaire ever miss an opportunity of being sad?

She was forever sighing: "I'm *so* unhappy!" We used to laugh at her for it. She would breathe the words plaintively, her sensitive hands pressed in above her waist, squeezing her strong, rounded little body, her high, wide-set ribs. "I've got ribs like an Empire bolero," she said. She sorrowed because the daylight faded or the rain fell; she was saddened by love, by her ambitions, her doubts, her thirst for everything that life could give, her simplicity. "And to think that I've got the lucky signs!" she would cry. "I've got the teeth that bring you happiness!" and she would display her healthy gums, her faultless white teeth and the little spaces between them. Happiness! O my dear, my poor, sad Polaire of 1935!

People still remember the success she made of the play. Against all likelihood she dressed the sixteen-year-old heroine, for the first act, in socks and a black overall, like a Poulbote drawing, and for the second, in a foaming white dress that was equally impossible. But the public adored everything she did. As she played it, the scene in the second act, where Claudine drinks a mite too much, became a thing of delicate fantasy, deliciously chaste and gay; she sailed blissfully through the banalities of the last act, danced over its pitfalls without so much as seeing them. How passionately she loved, she still loves, the stage! A visionary, a soul possessed.

I often went to see her in her dressing-room. If we did not go on to a tavern with M. Willy to eat her favourite supper, which was my favourite too—a big wedge of cheese with the knob of a round loaf and a glass of red wine—we would say goodbye at the stage door of the '*Bouffes*'. Already she was no longer the carefree, happy Claudine, her mood had darkened:

"Goodbye, Colette. Good night."

"Sleep well, Polaire."

"Oh I don't sleep much, you know. I lie and wait."

"Who for?"

"Nobody! I wait and wait for tomorrow's performance."

She was telling the truth. Every real passion has its ascetic side, and her passion for her art made Polaire neglectful of love. Her neglect was deeply mortifying to the handsome young man, the rich young 'blood', who loved 'Popo' in his simple, frank, sometimes rather brutal fashion.

She went so far as to banish Pierre L—— from 'her' theatre, even forbidding him, except on rare occasions, to come there at midnight and fetch her away.

"What would people say," she cried indignantly, "if gentlemen called for me here? They'd say I wasn't serious, they'd say I was only thinking of having fun!"

So she often went home alone, springing lightly into her victoria, when the weather was fine, her tiny toy-terrier clasped to her breast. Her carriage was drawn by two piebald horses, like something out of a fairy story or a travelling-circus, and away she drove, a strange young woman who had no need of true beauty to put all other women in the shade, an inspired actress to whom training and study were equally unnecessary. The hem of her pale-coloured dress swept like a curling wave about her ankles, hiding or curving up over her high, white boots —boots such as a hunting nymph might have worn, or a lion-tamer at a fair—and the passers-by turned to stare at 'Claudine'.

One night M. Willy was awakened by the violent ringing of the telephone. He lifted the receiver and heard a confused noise of sobs and muffled cries: "Vili! Oh Vili! . . . Come quick! I'm dying."

A short outburst of curses, and M. Willy leapt from his bed, flung a top-coat over his Russian-embroidered nightgown and hurried off, calling a few brief orders to me over his shoulder:

"Dress. Get there as soon as you can. I don't know what's up at Polaire's but it looks as if tonight's takings were bitched."

He found, we found, Polaire on the floor of her bedroom, half under the bed. Sitting on the bed and most admirably lit by a pink-frilled table-lamp, was a young man in pyjamas, Pierre L——. His eyes glowered, and with arms folded on his chest, he was breathing quickly through his nostrils like a boxer at the end of a round.

Down for the count, Polaire lay prostrate, if indeed the word prostrate can be applied to the stricken serpent, the frantic panther, to every live creature that can writhe and toss and buckle madly, tear the ground with its claws, sob, roar. The young man looked down at her in silence, motionless, making no attempt to help or soothe.

"Good God!" gasped M. Willy. "Whatever is the matter with her?"

Pierre L——'s handsome mouth remained grimly closed, but an answer issued, panting and incoherent, from underneath the bed:

"Vili! He hit me! . . . The brute! The brute! . . . Here . . . and here . . . and here! . . . Vili! I want to die! . . . Oh! Oh! Oh! Oh! I'm *so* unhappy! . . . Get a policeman! Get a policeman! I'll have him sent to prison! I'll have him put in irons!"

M. Willy wiped his forehead and enquired anxiously (first things first):

"Is she badly hurt?"

Pierre L—— shrugged his shoulders.

"Hurt? Don't be funny! A couple of wallops . . ."

The prostrate victim sprang to her feet. Crowned with curl-papers large as the largest Roman snails, puffed with tears, swollen with sighs and cries, she still glowed, in her long nightdress, like some fiery Eastern sorceress; nothing that was excessive or frenzied could ever make her ugly.

"A couple of wallops?" she repeated. "And what about this? . . . And this?"

She pointed to her arms, her neck, her shoulder, her thighs that were made to grip the bare flanks of a horse.

"The police!" she whispered childishly. "Call the police."

Tears of exhaustion and defeat overcame her, and she sank to the ground again. M. Willy, much relieved, sat down on the bed beside Pierre L——.

"My dear old fellow! This sort of thing isn't decent.

You must forgive me if I tell you, as a friend, that a decent-hearted man, a man of feeling . . ."

The dear old fellow laid a large, white, well-kept hand upon his unfeeling heart:

"In the first place I don't care a damn," he declared, "whether I'm decent or not. As for tonight—she said something I couldn't stand. No!" he suddenly shouted. "No! I can't and I won't stand it!"

He got up, scrabbling with his fingers in his thick, ash-gold hair.

"Can't you tell me what happened?" suggested M. Willy in a conciliatory tone. "You know you can trust me."

"She said——" began Pierre L—— at the top of his voice. "She said—that I wasn't gentle!"

Below him, on the carpet, Polaire stirred feebly, shook her cluster of monster snails, moaned.

"That—I—was—not—gentle!" Pierre L—— barked out. "When I heard that, I saw red. . . . Not gentle! I! I!"

He struck his fine chest with his fists.

"I——! Everybody knows it! I'm the mildest of men! *I* not gentle! . . ."

Groans came from the carpet, broken and despairing. . . .

"No, you're not. You're not gentle. . . . You don't understand anything. . . . You don't know what gentleness and understanding are. . . . What a woman really wants from love isn't what you think it is. . . . It's . . ."

"D'you hear her?" Pierre L—— thundered. "She's at it again! My God!"

He threw off his pyjama jacket, bent over the floor. M. Willy was about to intervene when two amber arms rose and closed about the smooth neck of the mildest of men.

"Pierre . . . I'm so unhappy. . . . Nobody loves me. . . . Pierre . . ."

"My little duck. . . . My lovey girl. . . . Popo darling. . . . Who said nobody loved you?"

He picked her up, held her, slung across his breast like a dark gazelle, carried her, humming softly, back and forth about the great Louis XV bed. M. Willy turned to me:

"I feel that our presence is no longer essential. But they did give me a turn! They're killing, don't you think?"

He wiped his forehead and laughed, but I could not do the same. Standing there, unwanted, almost in silence, I had had ample time to watch a strange, unknown sight—love in its youth and its violence, an outraged lover, naked to the waist, the silky woman's skin above the perfect muscles, the rippling play of light upon the proud, careless body, his easy assurance as he stepped over and then picked up the fallen body of Polaire.

I saw the back of his trim, well-shaped neck and the ash-gold hair falling like rain over Polaire's hidden face. Her arms about him, he rocked his victim gently, and she had forgotten we were there.

"Hey! Young Pierrot! Can you promise not to try our star's nerves too hard? Not to give her advice so—er—convincingly?"

The young head lifted and we saw the flushed, ferocious face, the mouth still moist from the interrupted kiss.

"Only when it's absolutely necessary, old man. I promise . . ."

I joined M. Willy who, by way of being funny, was tripping to the door on tiptoe, and we went out.

M. Willy, his mind now entirely at rest, seemed greatly

amused by our night's adventure. I was not so entertained.

"Are you cold? You don't want to go home on foot, do you?"

No, I was not cold. Yes, I was cold. All the same I would have liked to go home on foot. Or not to go home at all. Walking beside him, I looked back in my mind at the room we had just left. I can see something of it still—highlights of pale blue against a dim background, lamps that shone pink in their little embroidered shades, the tumbled, white expanse of a lover's bed. I have kept the memory of a prolonged, uneasy sadness that I ought, perhaps, to call jealousy.

From the day when, following M. Willy's instructions, I cut off my too long hair, a number of clever people discovered that I bore a strong likeness to Polaire. Unless twin sisters are dressed in identical clothes and do their hair in the same way, clever people seldom exclaim at their striking resemblance. It is true that Polaire's ears and mine were set very far from the nose and that our eyes were perfectly level. But indeed I envied the beauty of her eyes as much as I envied her ankles, her teeth, her delicate little ears.

To be strictly honest, I must admit I was not sorry to lose the great inconvenient rope of hair that was weighing me down, feeding on my strength. Once rid of it, the only thing that spoilt my pleasure was a letter from "Sido". She rebuked me in strangely grave terms: "Your hair was not your own. It was mine, the work of twenty years of care and attention. You have disposed of a precious trust that I had confided to you."

But I shook a happy head, freed from its burdens and its pins, and cried joyfully to myself: "I can feel the air! I can feel the air tickling my scalp!" Beside me, someone infinitely more far-seeing was otherwise concerned; M. Willy was busy inventing a pair of twins.

Under his direction, Polaire and I were fitted out with three precisely similar costumes—only three, but that was quite enough, that was altogether too much. There was a tartan suit in black and brown and green; there was a white dress and a hat of the sort known as a 'Charlotte', in white tulle with bunches of cherries; there was a second coat and skirt in greyish blue with bands of greyish white and tabs and stitching and heaven knows what ribbed braidings that the tailor called 'straps' and that led, during one of our early fittings, to a slight confusion. The cutter explained:

"This is where the straps tail off. They have got to be stitched."

Polaire, who had, as usual, been lost in her own thoughts, suddenly woke up:

"Oh! Poor little creatures! Oughtn't you to bandage them as well?"

Her mind and the situation having been cleared up, she apologised:

"I thought a 'straps' was a little dog. Rather like a fox-terrier, but much smaller."

On the days when our manager took us out to restaurants in our 'twins' disguise, she was constrained, sad as a dressed-up animal is sad, and her shrinking made people stare and smile yet more maliciously. She could not hide it; Polaire always put her whole soul into her face. Mine was not so easily read; no signs of a decent embarrassment could be detected there! I was thirty; I had had ten years training.

I am sure that Polaire remembers the night of a dress rehearsal at one of the music-halls—Moulin Rouge? Casino de Paris? Folies Bergère?—at which we were "on duty".

"Put on your white frocks," said M. Willy. "I'll look as if I were trotting out my two kids."

As the three of us went into the stage-box, the audience focussed its attention on us with such intensity, a feeling so unanimous, so silent, so heavy, that Polaire's sensitive antennae caught it and quivered. She took a quick step back, as though a trap had opened.

"Well Popo? What is it?" our manager asked.

She was clinging with both hands to the door of the box, trying to slip away: "No . . . no . . . I don't want to . . . Please, please . . . I can hear what they're thinking—it's ugly, it's horrible."

She gave in, of course. But as she presently sat beside me in the blazing lights, sighing out her: "I'm *so* unhappy," I was very very sorry for her that night.

After the run of *Claudine à Paris*, M. Willy, determined to draw every likely covert, to suck every spring dry, engaged Polaire to act *Le p'tit jeune homme*, and *Le Friquet*, a play taken from a novel by Gyp. But in her dinner jacket and fancy waistcoat, a Panama hat on her exuberant hair, Polaire was not happy. Although slimmer than any woman ever has been, she detested playing men's parts and wore her clothes with so little zest that they gave her the look of a sick Brazilian boy. Like all gentle, sensitive animals, Polaire always seems ailing when she is sad. Sadness makes her draw in her elbows, clasp her hands, droop her cheek upon her shoulder, like those ravishing little monkeys that the dealers in exotic animals bring to our cold shores to die. Playing *Le p'tit jeune homme*, creating the part of *Le Friquet*, Polaire pined for Claudine. The bitterness of her regret, her intense nostalgic longing, gave an extraordinary and as it were posthumous life to the figure I had invented and by whom I, personally, was not deceived. But Polaire's belief in Claudine, her feeling for Claudine, her thoughts of her, were deep and pure. A revival of the play, or a tour with it in the provinces, awakened an almost mystical response. "I am going to *her*," she would say. She speaks of Claudine now as of a beloved friend she has lost. Her faith, her certainty were such that secretly

I withdrew, I bowed down, I gave Polaire the credit of having invented Claudine.

Other actresses took up the part later; it had a singular fascination for a whole generation of young players. Even where it does not tempt the spectator, the 'unripe fruit', the acid charm of the girl dressed as a child but free to behave as a woman, goes strangely to the performer's head and makes her over-estimate her own gifts. So it happened that we were given Claudines of every shape and colour, Claudines that were blonde, brunette and red-haired, lanky, squat, husky and consumptive. One even had a beard, Eva L——, a pathetic child who acted with delicacy and perception and was, indeed, the best, after Polaire. She was the daughter of a genuine, official 'Bearded Woman', and was afflicted, like her mother, with a terrible growth of blue-black hair that ruined her looks in a couple of hours. By day she wore a thick veil; in the evening she would shave before making up. But by midnight a blueish smoke had begun to show through the cosmetics, smudging her cheeks and chin, reasserting her infirmity, bringing her, at last, to irremediable despair.

But, as Polaire had asserted after she had read the play and before she was given the part—"No, Monsieu-eur Vili, *I* am the real Claudine!"—there was never but one player whose every movement was so alive with vehemence and fire, whose face had so true a fervour, whose voice could tremble and half choke with such natural emotion that all thoughts of schooling, technique, deliberate sensuality were blown to the winds—there was never a 'real Claudine' but Polaire.

How old was I? Twenty-nine, thirty?—the age when life musters and arrays the forces that make for duration, the age that gives strength to resist disease, the age when you can no longer die for anyone, or because of anyone. Thirty already—and already that hardening which I would compare to the crust that lime-springs form, dripping slowly. One by one the warm drops trickle from the forehead to the feet, and you are scared: "Why! It is blood! It is my blood!" But it is not blood, it is the petrifying water slipping down, leaving, as it dries, a fine, powdery ash that gradually thickens. So do the aged crabs put on their coats of lime and the old, old lobsters, dozing underneath the rocks, grey and stony and almost invulnerable. I was very far from invulnerable, but I had no wish to die. As long as "Sido" was alive I could never have dreamed of killing myself. And even if I set aside, as best I can, the thought of "Sido" and try to picture my youth without her, I do not believe that suicide and I would ever have confronted or attracted one another. I do not like things that are easy, and as for our deaths being well-timed, only other people can judge of that, and indeed usually do so with much wisdom and unction: "He died in good time." "Ah! poor woman! She chose the right moment."

Thirty, then, or thereabouts, and the wish to endure, the habit of endurance that grew with the growing shell and the daily tests I challenged myself to face. Ten years of Paris, and, appearances notwithstanding, a most singular state of isolation. Two people were responsible for creating and maintaining this condition, M. Willy and I. M. Willy "knew a good many people", a large public rather than individuals. We went about a great deal but were seldom invited privately. What 'sound, respectable' background had we to recommend us? Only one as far as I can see, my husband's family, and it opened and closed its doors to us by fits and starts, timorously. The 'Society' stage of M. Willy's career came later.

Together we aroused considerable curiosity; by myself I aroused no interest of any kind. I could not have put a name to two hundred faces. The unsociable tendency natural to all "Sido's" children, had something to do with it, but M. Willy's deliberate, concealed purpose must also be taken into account. In the summer he consigned me to a protective solitude; in Paris I could not but see how carefully he restrained every youthful, friendly impulse I might have towards men and women of my own age. Such impulses were not frequent, but he always curbed them decisively and with consummate skill. If my sympathy—which always wore an abrupt, ungracious air, making no show of eagerness or the wish to please— appeared to welcome a woman's smiling invitation or a man's veiled warmth, M. Willy was instantly aware of it. "That is not a friend for you," he would say, gently reproving; "such a friendship is unworthy of you," and he never failed to give the very serious grounds for his strictures. Where necessary, he would add in his most graceful manner: "I am a little jealous, you know, of my proud little girl." Not so much of a little girl, and, alas! very far from proud, and as for jealousy! He seemed to know that the promptings of friendship would work more powerfully against him than those of love, and also that friendship, which is of its nature a delicate thing, fastidious, slow of growth, is easily checked, will hesitate, demur, recoil where love, good old blustering love, bowls ahead and blunders through every obstacle. Love comes disguised as a thunderbolt and often vanishes at the same pace. Twenty years are not too long to shape a friendship, to ensure its present and its future safety. Dear friends of twenty years and over, of ten years or less, I will not speak of you here; we like to meet in the quiet places, away from the bright lights and the din. Take care of yourselves, live longer than I do. Thank you.

Youth often gets the friendships it deserves. The young people who read this and who happen to be bleeding from a wounded friendship will protest and swear I am unjust. But I did not make this criticism in my extreme youth.

When I married I had no adolescent affection to betray, no close link such as so often binds two girls together, apeing marriage as playful animals ape the ways of love, that is awkwardly, gaily, with laughter and sometimes an ignorant and vindictive violence of feeling. Village life does not allow for secrets and, though it cannot prevent the birth of such intimacies, it hinders them, laughs at them and finally discourages them altogether. As for those I might have known after marriage, I was at first inclined to be hostile. Not that I disliked women particularly, but I was boyish and at ease in the society of men and feared women rather as I would have feared any luxury that required care and a certain wariness.

Thirty, then, and a most unusual dearth of feminine companions, of feminine complicity and support. The ideal accomplice, the true helper, I had them both in "Sido", in "Sido" so far away and yet so near. Every week I wrote her two or three long letters, full of news of things that had happened, or not happened, of descriptions, of boasting, of trifles, of myself, of her. She died in 1912. Still, now, twenty-three years later, I sit down at my table, or at a hotel writing-desk if I am travelling, and pull off my gloves and ask for picture-postcards with 'views of the neighbourhood' which were the sort that she liked best. And why should I stop writing to her? Why be checked by such a futile, vainly questioned obstacle as death?

Thirty. . . . Was I regretting the early years, the first hovels, the 'Bohemian' life and its odd, attorney's office setting, my long, lazy days in the half dark, my convalescence on the divan-bed that had been embroidered in tapestry stitch by my predecessor? I had nothing against this unknown woman but her love of sewing large, sharp-edged spangles at intervals on the thick canvas. I missed the fits of giggles that used to break through the day's gloom. I remembered Pierre Veber, who had quarrelled with my husband over the business of *Une Passade*, and missed his boisterous good humour. But moods of that kind cannot last for ever anyway, the wild high spirits that play-act for their own amusement as much as to astound the gallery, the boyish absurdity that sent Pierre Veber rushing full tilt, his walking-stick clattering ahead of him, down the three flights of our Rue Jacob staircase. From the courtyard he shouted up at M. Willy:

"There is a law, Sir! There are judges who deal with people who chuck their creditors downstairs instead of paying their debts!"

Every window of the old house opened, including ours. Two long pigtails leaned out, and a vast, shining, naked brow. M. Willy, taking his cue, replied at the top of his voice:

"My creditors, Sir? I respect my creditors! I honour them! I am a conscientious and punctilious debtor! I value my creditors! But I will not give that decent name to a dirty little squit who comes after me twice a week on the pretence that I owe him thirty-two francs but in fact to pinch my cook's behind!"

The concierge, conceived and created in the old tradition, her broom at her side, her cotton jacket bursting from her skirt, drunk with cheap rum and grocer's Chartreuse, applauded her tenant loudly:

"That's knocked him!"

Meanwhile Paul Masson glided through the crowd that had instantly assembled, his brief-case under his arm, distributing pictures, that were not of a devotional nature, with criminal impartiality to schoolboys and schoolgirls alike. "To while away the long winter evenings," he whispered.

By this time we had reached the 177 *bis* of the Rue de Courcelles, and I was making a fair copy of *La Retraite Sentimentale*, reviving my acute grief for its 'Casamène', that is for the Monts-Boucons. At 177 *bis* I also wrote a first version of *Minne*, which was a story of fifty or sixty pages that I had painted in the colours I liked, red, pink, black, and a few touches of pale gold on the little heroine. My story was half fantasy, half news' item; it had come to me—mildly sophisticated and making fun of its own 'literary' airs—from the neighbouring fortifications, and I had wanted to keep it to myself, to sign it with my own name as I had signed the *Dialogues des Bêtes*. But M. Willy would not allow it. From an unrelenting, unceasing assault, a siege that would have broken the stoutest heart, I retired beaten. I stretched *Minne* out into a novel; I calmly made her adulterous in *Les Egarements de Minne*. Later, I fought to get her back, but I had striven more bitterly before I let her go. I have turned the two books into one, knitted them together; I shall never see again the pleasant little face 'Minne' had before her 'growing pains.' It may be said that, for the honour of the French novel, it is as well that the end of my cowardice cut her career short and nipped in the bud God knows what *Minne in Hell, Minne's Daughter, Minne's Divorce*.

It was an odd place, that second storey of a private house, at 177 *bis*. The first floor sheltered a single, silent neighbour, Prince Alexander Bibesco. I used to look out sometimes and watch the beautiful red and gold hair of Princess Bibesco (née Hélène Reyer, the first and most touching 'Claudinet' in *Les Deux Gosses*) go down the winding staircase like a torch flung down a well. The flat was different from any I had known. We had gone to it from a little studio at No. 93 in the same street that was in the very worst artistic taste, painted in hospital green, furnished with white goatskin rugs that professed to be bearskins, delirious with every shade of green, with a frenzy of Bing ornaments, a pretentious infatuation for the vitreous and the tubby, and embellished with two excommunications launched against M. Willy by Erik Satie.

A bourgeois menace lurked in every corner of 177 *bis*. I bore it with a curious apathy, but I felt I was losing self-confidence, as though personally threatened.

M. Willy had acquired, in settlement of a bad debt, a 'complete' bedroom suite, so complete, in fact, that its woven cane and white lacquer were encrusted with oval medallions of imitation Wedgwood at every point, on the panels of the bed and of the wardrobe, on the backs of the chairs, on the dressing-table and its triple mirror. The dressing-table in question boasted three drawers, set in waist high, especially designed for containing jewellery. Having no jewellery, I used them to store my collection of glass marbles, a collection which, through all vicissitudes of fortune, storms and stresses, journeys, changes of address and of civil status, I have managed to preserve and even to enrich.

Dully, as though unheedingly, I allowed the deplorable furniture to settle in my home and made no protest, did not react beyond a secret start of amazement and disbelief: "This is not possible, it can't be true. I don't *really* live here."

A lady's maid, who came to supplement the efforts of the cook, gave me the same feeling of fantastic unreality. She had a wall eye, a familiar attachment to the word 'incommensurable', the gift of taking locks to pieces and putting them together again, and an obvious delight in her own mystery. What she was hiding seemed harmless and comical compared with what I had feared. For a series of accusing letters presently enlightened me: Louisa was writing obscene verses to all the servant girls of the neighbourhood, and our own cook brought us, in great indignation, a little ode in which her dark charms were celebrated with delectation and concupiscence. Beneath her signature the poetess had added: "*P.S. I'll go to a hundred francs, Antonine. It's not a joke. I mean it.*"

Louisa of Mitylene departed, exquisitely shameless, a smile upon her lips. I watched the people and the seasons go and come, pass away; I worked, I looked after a home of which the worst that can be said is that it lacked a soul. A fugitive soul. Perhaps it was mine, seeking its salvation?

I did not dare, I did not wish to come to any sudden, violent decision. Having accepted, once in the middle of the summer, that my stay at the Monts-Boucons should not have left the Paris flat empty of female company, I had taken the full measure of my cowardice and had made certain also of my flexibility, which is the name I have always given to my self-control, being convinced that no human resistance can stand fast if it cannot sometimes yield. My prolonged delay, my prolonged terror do not please me, certainly, but I would be lying if, to make a show of crying *"Mea Culpa!"*, I called them a waste of time.

I had begun by rejecting women's friendship, by refusing to hear its unnecessary appeal. I believed, I felt myself too strong, and also ill-equipped, unfitted for a confidential relationship. And a little 'proud' in the sense that my part of the country gives to the word. Nothing was easier than to sit round a table at the 'Vachette' with the little Loutes and Moutes and Touffes of the Latin Quarter and to laugh with them and listen to their laughter, but one day it occurred to M. Willy to bring home a lively young model of Léandre's, the notorious Fanny Z——, and this time I did not laugh at all.

Art-lovers, that year, were greatly taken with a panel Léandre had painted (Gustave Lyon bought it) of Fanny Z—— in profile, upright in her black, wicked-angel's dress. When I saw her in my flat, her soft chestnut hair tumbling on her shoulders, when I saw her toss her page's toque on to my bed and move about my room, touching everything in it with her lovely, tip-tilted fingers, putting out her tongue before my mirror, when I saw her open her frock in a casual, accustomed manner on her naked, eager breasts and heard her explain to M. Willy, to me, to the birds at the open window, what she enjoyed most in the way of voluptuous practices, the blood of 'Madame Colette's daughter' rebelled. I made the same tight-lipped face I used to make at the first sign of 'callers' and used to run and hide 'proudly' in the top branches of the tallest tree. Precisely the same pinched, prudish face.

"Come on now," grown-up people say to children. "Give her your hand, give him a kiss, go and have a nice game." But the children stand there, silent and stiff as icicles, blushing and deeply offended, and will not budge. M. Willy's urbanity did not improve matters, not at least between Fanny Z—— and myself. But she was too much taken up with her own interests that day to notice anything.

In young women, marriage—a first marriage anyway —does not invariably wipe out all traces of the romantic schoolgirl. At twenty-two I suffered a sharp but brief infatuation for a great, red-haired horse of a woman, heavily dyed, who taught the piano. A sudden 'crush', the affection a pupil feels for a teacher. And this teacher was all darkness and red gleams, sea-green Liberty damasks, Juliet caps richly embroidered with glass beads. As for her name, I prefer not to set it down rather than confess that it was Daffodyl, Aglavaine, or Ortrude.

Every period shapes its particular type of woman in the manner of some artist, but never of an artist who is really great. My Liberty lady was a Rops. The useless memory that recalls details with infallible precision, having stripped her of her aquarium colours and adornments, shows her to me once again, high cheek-boned, huge of hip, with a pale, leek-green eye, like the fairheaded slaughtermen Jean Lorrain loved so well. When she discovered that I knew Jean Lorrain she fell, or pretended to fall, into a swoon of ecstasy and begged for the honour of an introduction. He consented and immediately took his revenge. He spent five minutes with her at my flat, looked her uncharitably up and down and went off, signing to me to follow him. On the landing he caught me by the arm and put his lips close to my ear.

"You fool!" he whispered. "Can't you see she is a man?"

And left me there, aghast.

A few weeks later he laughed at me for being so credulous and swore he had only been joking. But I had seized the first opportunity of bidding farewell to the lady whose name was Alladine or Joyzelle.

WHEN I met Jean Lorrain, the lusty lad from Normandy was already losing his beauty and his strength. He liked to be known as 'the lad', but easily dispensed with it on closer acquaintance. I had been much struck by the carefully arranged henna-red lock he wore upon his forehead, between two streaks of white and the darker regions beyond, and had told him that his tricolour hair made him look like one of those three-coloured, tortoiseshell cats that are known as 'Portuguese'. He had been highly tickled by the comparison, and often signed the little notes he wrote me, after we had become friends, "The Portuguese Cat". Our friendship was frequently interrupted, sometimes by long intervals of time, yet it was always precious to me, coming as it did in the days when I was secretly unhappy at being no more than myself, that is to say a nice little woman who had no respect for her anonymous task and her submission. Merely by pointing to some detail in the way I did my hair, or to the narrow tie I wore, and saying "No, not like that, like this. That's better. And don't put red round your neck. Try and find a colour that matches your eyes", he had given me real pleasure.

It was easier for him to tell a woman of the fatigue, the physical distresses that tormented him and of the temperamental failings to which he was prone. He had remained curiously young and fresh in spirit, sensitive to the play of light and colour, enraptured by every landscape, southern landscapes especially. Such bad taste as he had was satisfied by jewellery of the cheaper sort, the less precious, clouded stones—chalcedony, chrysoprase, opal, olivine—and monstrous gold rings, abominably convoluted, that were quite impossible but that he wore nevertheless. He affected walking-sticks made of tortoiseshell, or heavy staffs such as drovers carry, strung with leather thongs; he loved blue scarves, blue handkerchiefs, flax-blue shirts, buttonholes of blue irises, for the sake of the vigorous blue life that such things gave to his own blue eyes. For it is true that, set in their yellowing whites, between lids that were reddened and inflamed, Lorrain could boast the finest blue eyes that ever shone in a man's face. Insatiable eyes, thirsting for every loveliness. His other features were not so remarkable. The short, slightly bovine nose and heavy chin of the person who jumps too quickly to conclusions, the high-coloured complexion that had become unhealthily blotched and that he tried to disguise by various clumsy means. Yet beneath the white crust of the make-up, beneath the raven-blue lines that he pencilled, towards the end, about his swollen, watering eyes, in the shadow of the huge, miller's hat that used to alarm the passers-by, I can still see, quite easily, the face of a man.

To the day of his death Jean Lorrain never gave up his right and his wish to be a fighter, not to say a brawler. When the chance of a quarrel or a duel arose he became entirely virile; he flung himself head foremost—the typical bull nature—into all the worst disputes and came out of them badly but full of truculence.

His handwriting is sadly revealing. Usually it slopes so extremely as to be almost level with the line, yet every now and then it stands up, stiff and straight, to record some piece of childishness or swagger. His letters awakened my first desire for the unknown Mediterranean, and seeing the word 'Marseille' sketched by his staggering pen, I saw, too, spread out before me, the great lazy stars that dance so softly, at midday, on the syrupy waters of the port. Affectionate letters, letters that are full, at first, of literary conceits and coyness, deliberately cynical, letters that little by little shrink and fade, letters that are dear to me, portraits of Jean Lorrain by Jean Lorrain.

"*Oh! yes, a tanned skin makes blue eyes bluer, but love in Provence paints the lids darker than in any place on earth!*

"*A bosom flushed with caresses
A bloom of amorous joy upon the lids* . . .

"*So I come back to you, but only to go away—again! Oh! the white sugar of the Exhibition after the apse of Saint-Trophime, the domes of the Trocaderrierro after the domes of Avignon, the purple face of Madame X—— that old strawberry dipped in champagne, after the ivory and green amber skins of Provence. Rage and jealousy will make you crave, Colette, most furiously for my death, I have come back so rich in sunshine and blue skies. All my most Lorraine affection.*

"*I have been drinking and revelling and all the rest of it! Such a lot of Claudes and such a lot of Claudines. I don't suppose you'd care to know where I spent the night? This is boasting, my dear, but one must cultivate one's legend.*

*Prawns, very thoroughly cooked
Entrecôte Béarnaise
Sweet omelette with quince jelly
Bananas (only one)
and St. Galmier.*

"*Therrre, Colette! And the laughter of the Vieux Port and the kindness of young Mistral, who is a friend of mine. But this *evening . . . rice-water and camomile tea and bed at eight. . . . I would much rather be showing you round the Marseille hells. Tomorrow will see me in the Allées. The mornings there are delicious, bright sun and dark shadows.* Yours. *Herewith the piece the 'Gaulois' has turned down. Don't lose it for me. Quite a few sailors have given me the glad eye. And—'pon my word!—quite a few of the fishwives too. I am betrothed three times for tonight! Ah! if one only had the health! But I must go and grind out some more copy. . . . Your Lorrain-late-Phocas.*

" *'What a bore I'm going to be!'* "

One short note seems like a farewell. It is undated, a pale scrawl, a mere scratch on the paper in the yellowish ink of some hotel or hospital:

" *. . . I am very ill, very sick, deeply stricken. . . . I have chucked the 'Raitifs'. I have chucked 'Poussières', I can hardly hold my pen. I want to lie down in a corner, like a dog. I can no longer read.*

"*If you knew the depths of indifference my life has come to, or rather is slipping into, you would pity—or envy—your*

Jean Lorrain.*"*

Reading this message I had already begun to grieve . . . when I ran into him outside Laffitte, the Marseille bookseller, looking younger than ever, doped, freshly made-up, restored, once again, by the pink and green twilight that absolves the soul, in those lands, from every anxiety. But his underlip droops from time to time and quivers and grows moist.

"Come along! I'll show you a pretty house. Such a lovely staircase!"

He blows a kiss, his fingers to his poor, unruly lip. And off we go through narrow streets, past doorways where voices call his name occasionally in the typical

Marseille accent, "*Jain!*" until we come to a flight of steps and balusters of white marble, white as sugar, tortuous and Italian.

"Pretty?"

"Rather pretty. Shall we go back now?"

"Not till we've had a drink."

On the first floor he pushes his way through a door covered in sham leather beyond which the Madame, severe in black faille, also cries out "*Jain!*" and flings up her hands in welcome. Gold flashes from them—gold rings, gold bracelets, gold in solid bands, gold in thick chains. In the genteel drawing-room, four identical chromolithographs hang on the walls, celebrating the identical glories of the same pink bathing girl. I am chuckling over them as the door opens and 'the ladies' come in.

Authentic 'ladies'. Every now and then I beckon them over to me to make sure that nothing has been changed, no detail lost, that their helmets of shining hair still bear crests of ribbon, upright bows in the colours of the French flag, that their singular garment of coarse muslin, shaped like a flattened sentry-box, still covers them from head to foot.

Under the starched austerity of their gowns, they are, as custom prescribes, naked, but you can scarcely make out the great dark circles of the breasts, the harsh, still darker triangles, the red, white and blue garters on their black stockings. Three of them bow to me with stiff formality, but the fourth retires and sits down by the wall, and I cannot take my eyes off her and her wild mane of hair, standing like a cloud about her head, her staring, appalled face that has no nose.

"Crème de Menthe? Picon and lemon?" suggests Jain

The three clap their hands:

"Crème de Menthe! Crème de Menthe!"

Jain tries to persuade the fourth, but she sits like a blind woman, staring before her.

"Eh! Jain! Leave her alone."

The speaker represents, with much ease and fluency, the indigenous and social element of the community. She is thin, and has big breasts, a faintly hairy upper lip and the stern little eyes of the conscientious worker.

"Is she new?" Jain asks.

"You can say she's new if you like. Don't bother about her. She's not the sort for you."

The social lady settles her thick-meshed cage under her low, discreet bottom, and proceeds to make polite conversation:

"So you are just passing through, Madame? Eh! but it's a fine town, isn't it? And even in the heat there's always a nice sea breeze. And you can't say there aren't plenty of fine monuments, I'm sure."

"What's her name?" Jain insists. He, too, cannot keep his eyes off the noseless girl.

The loquacious lady's dignity sags a little:

"Eh! If I told you she's sometimes called Mimi and sometimes called Augusta, you wouldn't be any the wiser! She can't even talk French!"

She sips her green drink delicately, wipes her mouth with the tips of her fingers and condescends to explain.

"She's been taken on for the coloured sailors."

A protesting hand raised, she adds quickly:

"But she doesn't work on this floor! Good gracious no! Only in the room downstairs, on the yard. Must you really be going? Now that you've found your way, Madame, I hope we'll have the pleasure . . . Eh! Jain! When will you be bringing me that bottle of Chypre? It's over a year since you promised! Hoping to see you again, Madame. . . . Hey, Jain! Leave her alone, can't you! A dog'll give you its paw, but she doesn't even know that much."

I remember that, going down the handsome white staircase, stretched with crimson velvet paper, Jean Lorrain assured me, without deep conviction, that white and red have always incited men to love and pleasure.

"Men perhaps," I retorted sourly, "but good God, not women!"

I was longing for something that would taste fresh and sharp, for some place where there would be no gas lamps, no chromolithographs, no polite ladies; I longed for shellfish, for a sauce with vinegar and shallots in it.

More particularly I longed to forget the girl with the haggard, noseless face. But I was not allowed to. Dining at Basso's, Lorrain declared that she would make an admirable subject for a 'triptych' and went on volubly to transform her into an Egyptian donkey-boy, a snake-eater, finally a hermaphrodite, until I was sickened of her altogether. But after he had gone, she reasumed, in my mind's eye, her stiff muslin prison, her frozen ugliness, and returned to her fate—in the room downstairs, on the yard.

ABOVE the flat in the Rue de Courcelles, a narrow stairway led to a studio and a tiny bedroom. There were already many more studios in these days than there were painters, but the painters could find nowhere to paint in, the studios being all taken up by high-class lovers, eccentric ladies and even quite ordinary people who fought for the privilege of furnishing them with garden benches, divan-beds, Japanese umbrellas, Church vessels and choir stalls. Mine had no ornaments beyond the fittings of a gymnasium, the horizontal bar, trapeze, rings and knotted rope. I used to swing and turn over the bar, suppling my muscles half secretly, without any particular zeal or brilliance. Yet, when I reflected on it later, it seemed to me that I was exercising my body much in the way that prisoners, although they have no clear idea of flight, nevertheless tear up their sheets and plait the strands together, sew gold coins into their coat-linings, hide chocolate under the mattress.

For indeed I was not dreaming of flight. Where could I go? What could I live on? And "Sido", "Sido"! The thought of her was always with me and the obstinate determination never to go back to her, never to admit. It must be understood that I had nothing that belonged to me personally. And it should be realised, too, that captives, animals or men, are not constantly absorbed by the notion of escape, for all their restless pacing behind the bars and the way they have of gazing far away into the distance, through the encircling walls. The long glance, the unquiet step are only reflexes, brought about by habit or the size of their prison. Open the door that the bird, the squirrel, the wild beast have been eyeing, besieging, imploring, and instead of the leap, the sudden flurry of wings you expected, the disconcerted creature will stiffen and draw back into the depths of its cage. I had plenty of time to think, and I was constantly hearing the same grand, contemptuous, sarcastic words, shining links of a fine-wrought chain: "After all, you are perfectly free...."

Flight? But how do you set about flight? To 'desert the domestic hearth' was to us provincial girls of 1900 or so, a formidable and unwieldy notion, encumbered with policemen and barrel-topped trunks and thick veils, not to mention railway time-tables.

Flight? And what of the monogamous blood that ran in my veins, so inconveniently? It could never have breathed the word 'flight' with its hint of swift serpents darting through the grass. All I did was to fly from the so-called Dutch drawing-room, the second-hand bedroom, designed for economically-minded tarts, the bathroom that a former tenant had installed in a triangular wall-cupboard. Imagine a bath suitable for mammoths, a water-tank huge as a bastion and weights from a grandfather clock to measure the water level. Kiki-the-Demure and I repaired to the empty studio, where the battered plaster walls were, for some inexplicable reason, becoming more and more attractive to me every day. At times Boulestin joined me and we would hold pow-wows that had the hushed and secret air of conspiracies, but were, in fact, concerned with gossip, tittle-tattle about London and men's clothes. It is always useful for a woman to know how and why a man is well or badly dressed. Robert d'Humières would climb the three storeys, stride as it seemed lazily across the floor and fling himself down on the shabby little divan. Then, with a sudden, unexpected leap, he would be across the studio and standing upright on the trapeze, a feat that was followed, as in the case of cats, by an attitude of prim detachment. Occasionally other friends found their way to the comfortless attic without pausing on the second floor. I paid no particular heed to this new symptom, but nothing escaped M. Willy, who had not yet finished with the 'twins' idea and did not like to see me wasting my time on boys. Polaire's passionate vocation kept her increasingly bound to her beloved theatre; instinct, apprehension and a healthy repugnance made her avoid three-sided dinners and outings. M. Willy was a man of principle and subtlety; he started to shape an extra, a 'sub-twin'.

Mlle R——, a student at the *Conservatoire*, was chosen out of the throng of would-be Claudines. She had a taste for doing nothing, no talent for the stage, ash-blonde hair, very pale, and very fine eyes, a large nose, and looked more like Louis XV young than like Claudine or Colette. But two or three dresses and as many hats produced the required result, and public opinion did the rest. You will find fifty portraits of the young woman in a book signed Willy, entitled—quite simply—*Willy en bombe*, and illustrated with photographs. I have not read it. But I have looked at the pictures.

M. Willy sent the girl up to the studio-gymnasium so that, as he put it, she should limber-up a bit. She had a guileless nature and showed it guilelessly. When M. Willy took us out together in the victoria, he always put Mlle R—— in the children's place, the tip-up seat, where she sat looking faintly offended. One day she let out the reason for her sulky air: "Why must I always sit on the tip-up seat?" she said. "It isn't fair. We ought at least to take it in turns." This outburst made me laugh, but M. Willy, oddly enough, was angry: "I'm sick of her," he cried. "I can't stand the tiresome creature and her sad nose."

Was a nice match in twins becoming difficult to obtain? After Mlle R—— 's dismissal I heard no more of my chance impersonators, except indirectly. "M. Willy's daughter has bought a similar hat to yours," my milliner told me. Being already provided with a stepson, I was not going to quibble over a fancy stepdaughter. Another 'twin' remained forever unknown and unpaired, although she must have borrowed everything from me, including my name, since I presently received, after its flying career through many post-offices, a tender epistle from an assistant quartermaster-sergeant, written in a hand richly adorned with curls and flourishes, declaring that he could not bear to wait any longer for a "renewal of the divine moments enjoyed in the Circle train". He informed me further that he would wait for me "as he had done the first time", at the Brasserie de l'Espérance, Avenue de la Grande-Armée.

The discharge and banishment of Mlle R—— brought me back to the studio. While moving out of one flat and before settling in another, Marcel Boulestin camped for a few weeks in the tiny bedroom next door. Our friendship had leisure to develop and grow strong; it is still, like ourselves, of a sturdy complexion. Other affectionate bonds were formed without my seeking them. All about me, things and people were astir. If I had had a little more confidence, a firmer trust in Fate, a sharper gift of telepathy, I might have been aware of certain obscure commotions, hopeful signals, like those tapped on the walls by buried miners. One of the 'coloured-secretaries', as Boulestin amusingly called them—I will not give you all their names; some were highly specialised—a man I hardly ever saw, whispered to me one day: "If M. Willy tells you about his X scheme, don't have anything to do with it," and turned away hurriedly, his eyes cast down, like someone who had just slipped an anonymous note into the letter-box. Another time Paul Barlet, 'negro' in chief, emerged from the extreme shyness in which he had been enshrouded for ten years, to murmur, his voice a-quiver, his left knee shaking: "Madame! I have got all I could rescue of your manuscripts at my flat, Rue Fontaine. They are quite safe."

Freya, the clairvoyante, who was young in those days and at the outset of her fame and her career, looked at my hands and was astonished:

"It's . . . Oh! it's very odd. . . . I would never have thought it. . . . You must get out!"

"Of what?"

"Of where you are."

"The house I'm in?"

"Yes, but that's only a detail. You must get right out of it. You've lost a lot of time already."

With which pronouncement, for all the cryptic aspect of her diagnosis, I entirely agreed. Later I changed my mind and came to the conclusion that we were both wrong and that I had not lost too much time. It is better not to haggle over ten years of your life—I gave good measure and spent thirteen—provided they are youthful years. Later it is well to be thrifty.

Was it love that kept me there, in defiance of the signs and omens, waiting, waiting? Any answer I might give to this question, whether yes or no, would seem to me suspect. When a passion is really the first, it is hard to say: at this hour, of this blow, love died. The dream that brings back to you in sleep the poignancy of a vanished first love is the only dream that can rival the tenacity of the nightmare that haunts school-children and octogenarians—the dream of returning to school and facing the oral exam.

One thing is certain: the extraordinary man I had married possessed the gift and practised the policy of occupying a woman's thoughts, several women's thoughts, at every hour of the day, of tracing, imprinting, maintaining a track that could never be confused with other tracks. The traces that happiness leaves are not necessarily permanent. I know women who, after they had done with him, had only happy lives before them. They came near, it seemed, to crying out, like the lover of great music translated by mistake into a Gounod paradise: "Nothing but harps! Nothing but harps! Merciful Father! Give us something on the triangle and the clarinet and a few sharp discords, for pity's sake!"

Flight would have meant thinking out, organising a future. My improvident father had bequeathed me no sense of tomorrow, and "Sido", the faithful, had done no more than cast a frightened glance at the narrow ways by which her children would travel towards death. Like her, I was lacking in imagination, and also in the faith that upheld Polaire and inspired the apocalpytic formulas of which she was so fond: "It's when you're sunk under a hundred feet of muck that someone comes along and gets you out."

No one, so far, had come to get me out. It is true that mountains would not have been heavier or more difficult to move than I was, although you would not have thought so if you had seen me riding in the mornings on the hack at ten francs an hour that I hired twice a week. My horse cannot have found me much of a burden; I was growing thinner every day. I did not realise then that to lose weight without dieting, to suffer a mysterious volatilisation of the body's substance, deserves serious attention. I tightened my leather belt by a hole or so, I drew in the laces of my little ribbon stays as far as they would go. My thinness astonished me, but I did not feel I was near the end of my resources, I was so taken up, in those days, with the help that was coming to me prematurely, usefully, openly, in its beautiful human shape. Faces, minds, how clear you are to me!—the luminous and all too rare appearances of Marguerite Moreno, the familiar reserve of Robert d'Humières, the friendship of a granddaughter of the Marquis de Saint-Georges, who signed her work 'Henri de Lucenay' and who lived, poor and resigned, and wrote novels of strange and remote adventure, by the side of her meagre boarding-house fire. And the fair-haired girl who looked so radiantly like Bonaparte and was studying for the stage. Renée Parny has not forgotten our rough, happy companionship and how our equally vehement and intolerant spirits used to drive us into fierce arguments and violent physical agitation, like two boys confined in a narrow playground. On one occasion M. Willy, returning home, found a sort of ball upon the carpet, a wild tangle of feet and fists, two locked bodies eager to hit and hurt, fighting, as women do, with quick, awkward, clawing blows.

We had quarrelled "about nothing, for the fun of it"; moreover Renée Parny had said nasty things about my cat.

Music, too, brought help and varying counsel, now on this side, now on that. Music had been to me, in the early years, an experience that I endured like an ordeal, in fear and stress; it is one of the pleasures that a secret discouragement finds hard to bear. I needed all the strength of my well-trained nerves to withstand the furious tension, the assault of the strings, the shock of the orchestral masses. And my musical memory being extremely vivid (my brothers' was no less acute), I found it difficult, afterwards, to escape from the echoes, the melodies, the ghostly invasion. As I lay in bed and watched the spot of light that the street-lamp cast upon the ceiling dance and flutter its pale wings, my mind was full of song, my toes and jaw-muscles beat out the rhythms.

The dancing light, the flutter of the music's wing, the fragments of melody that haunted and evaded me in the night-time, have been replaced, little by little, by the more pressing appeal of words. The melodic and the written phrase both spring from the same elusive and immortal pair—sound and rhythm. To write, instead of composing, is to pursue the same search, but in a trance that is less intensely inspired and that has a lesser reward. If I had composed music instead of prose I should despise what I have done for forty years. For words are wearisome and worn, while the arabesques of music are forever new.

When it first came to me, I saw no especial meaning in my surrender, I did not realise that to accept each storm of beloved music as a delicious defeat, to close my eyes upon two spontaneous, springing tears, was to have taken, secretly, a step forward. Yet I welcomed the release and made of it a link between my loneliness and the world of men in which I had no life, no kin, in which I vegetated, vacant and invisible to many people, to others over conspicuous and in a dim way besmirched. In the conversations that went on above my head between the musically elect, I sometimes dared to intervene, to put in a word that meant merely: "I am here, I am listening", so that they should not think me deaf, dense, altogether outcast.

Truly great men are always the simplest. I cannot think, unmoved, of Fauré, or handle and re-read the gay little notes he wrote me. Playful, tender little notes. He was often tender in his wish to charm and to be charmed; to enjoy a friendship with him that had no ulterior motives, sought nothing, made no demands, was all the more precious. I am amazed, now, looking at the little yellowed pages. Did he then give thought to me so often? Did his hand, on which the supple skin was soft and creased like a loose-fitting glove, leave its august labours, its leisure, so readily to write to me? In twenty lines, just to make me laugh, he would be childish or mocking, would sketch a pen caricature of Tiersot, or tell me how, out of caprice, he had thrown over the presidency of a competition at Saint-Claude, would add a musical phrase to "Yes indeed!" beneath his "I kiss your ear!" or promise to come and "set the bell going and then the fork" with "adequate vigour". In making believe that he was not Fauré I followed the discreet and delicate custom practised by his disciples, Louis de Serres, Pierre de Bréville, Bagès, the singer, Déodat de Séverac—and the dark Debussy.

Their names bring back the memory of an evening long ago, the night of the first performance of *Schéhérazade*. Debussy, at the end of the concert, had not had his fill of Rimsky-Korsakov. His lips hummed, he made reedy noises through his nose trying to recover a theme on the oboes, he drummed with his fingers on the lid of the boudoir grand, echoing the deeper notes of the kettle drums. Still pursuing, he jumped to his feet, snatched up a cork and rubbed the window with it to imitate a pizzicato on the double-bass. So does the Satyr, erect on his goatlegs, his eyes fierce between the twisted horns, pluck his favourite briar from the thicket. Debussy had something of the followers of Pan. With the help of the piano

I sang him the passages he wanted, and his eyes lost their haunted look, glanced at me humanly, as though he saw me for the first time. "Good memory! Good memory!" he said, and my heart warmed. It seemed that he was calling to me: "Good morning! Good news!"

But the time always came when the portents faded and I returned to my well-concealed, unsettled life. No threats, no prayers were needed to urge me back or keep me there. Surely such obstinacy should have discouraged the shapers of my destiny and their dark messages? Already, as though they knew just how to please and excite me, they were making absurd and comical suggestions that carried auguries in doubtful taste, proposals smelling of the caravan and the big top. Without warning or preamble, I was asked:

"Will you take over a 'turn' with thirteen trained Russian greyhounds? The woman who trained them is dying in hospital. It's a ready-made job, you can just step into it. Everything's fixed up, the tours, the contracts, everything. And it would be quite your style."

I have forgotten the name of the envoy who let fall this balm, this dew, this temptation, this breath of the high-road, this scent of the circus. I shrugged my shoulders and refused even to see the thirteen greyhounds. Thirteen greyhounds, their fabulous necks outstretched, the curve of their bellies drinking in the air. And thirteen hearts to conquer. Disquiet, anxiety. It was all very well for me to shrink back into my scribe's virtue, my familiar, faithful fear, anxiety remained, working within me, for me. Thirteen greyhounds, a rampart, a family, a home. How did I ever let them go? Sadly, my regrets followed them in their circuitous and glorious course: "Perhaps another time."

But thirteen greyhounds, made in the image of speed

and flight—you cannot recover them once you have allowed them to slip by. They were adrift; my hand was worthy, I am sure, to gather them up. Not having found the courage to do so, I had to accept other allies—ridicule, for instance. It is a most potent adjunct! Without it, how could I ever have drawn attention to myself?

One fine afternoon, on a lawn at Neuilly, in the gardens of Miss Nathalie Clifford-Barney, I played one of the two parts in Pierre Louÿs' *Dialogue au soleil couchant*. The name of the other improvised actress was Miss Eva Palmer. She was an American and had the most miraculous long red hair. Only on my elder half-sister have I seen the wealth that poured from Eva's forehead to her feet. For the *Dialogue* she bound its amazing abundance in ropes about her head and put on a blue-green, more or less Greek tunic, while I felt I was the perfect Daphnis in terra cotta crêpe de chine, cut very short, a pair of Roman buskins and a wreath in the Tahiti style.

Eva Palmer, white as a sheet, stammered out her words. I was so stiff with stage-fright that the rolling "r's" of my Burgundy accent became positively Russian. Pierre Louÿs, author and guest, listened. Or perhaps he did not listen, for we were undoubtedly pleasanter to look at than to hear. But we believed that the whole of Paris under its sunshades and its hats, which were immense that year, had its eyes upon us. After the performance I plucked up the courage to ask Louÿs if "it hadn't gone too badly."

He answered gravely: "I have experienced one of the greatest emptions of my life."

"Oh! dear Louÿs!"

"I assure you! The unforgettable experience of hearing my work spoken by Mark Twain and Tolstoi."

Eva Palmer reddened beneath the red splendour of her

woven and interwoven tresses, and Pierre Louÿs murmured consolingly, added his mild praises to the praise of Miss Barney and her friends. But the next moment everyone had forgotten the Boston shepherdess and the Moscow herdsman; from behind a screen of foliage a naked woman had appeared, riding on a white horse, its strappings studded with turquoises—a new dancer whose name was already known among the studio and drawing-room cliques: Mata Hari.

She was a dancer who did not dance much, yet at Emma Calvé's, before the portable altar that she used as a background, supported by a little group of coloured attendants and musicians and framed in the pillars of a vast, white hall, she had been sufficiently snake-like and enigmatic to produce a good effect. The people who fell into such dithyrambic raptures and wrote so ecstatically of Mata Hari's person and talents must be wondering now what collective delusion possessed them. Her dancing and the naïve legends surrounding her were of no better quality than the ordinary claptrap of the current 'Indian turns' in the music hall. The only pleasant certainties on which her drawing-room audiences could count were a slender waist below breasts that she prudently kept hidden, a fine, supple moving back, muscular loins, long thighs and slim knees. Her nose and mouth, which were both thick, and the rather oily brilliance of her eyes did nothing to alter—on the contrary—our established notions of the Oriental. It should be said that the finale of her dance, the moment when Mata Hari, freed of her last girdle, fell forward modestly upon her belly, carried the male—and a good proportion of the female—spectators to the extreme limit of decent attention.

In the May sunshine, at Neuilly, despite the turquoises, the drooping black mane of hair, the tinsel diadem and especially the long thigh against the white flanks of her Arab horse, the colour of her skin was disconcerting, no longer brown and luscious as it had been by artificial light but a dubious, uneven purple. Having finished her equestrian parade, she alighted and wrapped herself in a sari. She bowed, talked, was faintly disappointing. It was much worse on the day Miss Barney invited her as an ordinary guest to a second garden-party.

"Madame Colette Willy?"

A loud, strongly-stressed voice, calling me by my fancy name, made me turn round. I found a lady in a black and white check suit, her breasts held high by a boned cuirass of stays, a veil with velvet chenille dots upon her nose, holding out a hand tightly gloved in white glacé kid stitched with black. I also remember a frilled shirt with a stiff collar and a pair of shoes of a bright egg colour. I remember my amazement.

The lady laughed heartily, displaying a set of strong, white teeth, gave me her name, wrung my hand, expressed the hope that we might meet again and did not move a muscle as the voice of Lady W—— rose beside us, saying in clear, plain words:

"She an Oriental? Don't be silly! Hamburg or Rotterdam, or possibly Berlin."

The same summer another garden saw me, almost as shy and awkward as the first time, on another improvised stage. The spectators were scattered here and there beneath the trees, and I introduced myself to them, in verse, from the top of a platform:

> *I am a faun, so small and slim,*
> *Lusty and shapely, light of limb,*
> *My eye is soft, my smile has grace*

*I know, for when thirsty, if I look
In the clear mirror of the brook
Among the reeds I see my face.*

The little play, which was attributed to Willy but had been written by the most expeditious of his henchmen (he has produced other, infinitely better poetry), was ordered, composed, delivered and rehearsed inside a week.

"If it amused you to act in a real theatre," M. Willy said to me shortly after, "I have another sketch, in prose. In fact I am sure that it would be easy for you to organise a series of performances, of pleasant little trips. Brussels, for instance, is always interested in certain forms of entertainment, in well-known people."

The formal, 'newspaper-article' style of this communication, the cautious, neutral tone in which it was delivered, were enough to raise my alarms; I stiffened into utter silence, deepest attention to hear the remainder of the speech:

"And on the other hand it would provide an excellent opportunity of getting rid of this wearisome flat and of finding an adequate arrangement better suited to a different kind of life—oh! just slightly different. There's no hurry."

I could not possibly be mistaken, what I had heard was a dismissal. While I had been dreaming of flight, close beside me someone else had been planning to turn me quietly out of the house—out of my own house. But this time I was not asked if I were willing. Hastily, confusedly I tried to think, to decide. . . . Could I leave it so, could I endure this quiet, these few words? In our heart of hearts we all love loud cries and gestures that hit the ceiling.

I remember the flush that crept over my cheeks, I

remember my stupidity. Deprived by fraud of something I had wished to leave by stealth, I could only repeat to myself, again and again, the words of the Napoleonic Code: "to desert the domestic hearth"—words that did not seem to me unpleasant yet were big with a vague sense of disorder in the field, suggestive of pickets abandoning their posts, of hurried first-aid, words and actions that made me hesitate. The spirit of contradiction is as strong in a woman as her possessive instinct. If she has nothing in the world but her suffering she will cleave to her suffering. She will bury a brass ha'penny deep in the ground, she will grasp at walls that are crumbling, roofless.

"There's no hurry. . . ." What I had heard was: "It is all over." I would have liked to be the one to say. "It is all over." Since I had said nothing I could only hold my peace. From the moment of that "there's no hurry", I distinctly saw the hours rush by. I clung to what I planned to disrupt. In ten years I had not waited so consciously or so shamefully. I waited another week, another fortnight; I waited for some final thing, knowing that it would not be I who would put an end to my abjection but the man who had first had his way with me. And still the same mildness, the same absence of noise, a silence as of falling snow. Before that moment I could have pictured an elopement as well as anyone else—the white plume of the departing train if not the galloping of splendid horses, a goodbye letter, breathing peace and goodwill, truly noble-hearted, a scarf fluttering in the wind, all the romantic glories of running away, alone or in company. But I could not make eviction lyrical. It can be so, however. I discovered that later, in the little ground-floor flat in the Rue de Villejust.

It was there that I faced the first hours of a new life,

between my dog and my cat. I had also brought away with me my old, faithful fear; it remained faithful for a long while. At every ring of the bell—a real bell with a real clapper and an intolerable, sharp voice, like an orphanage bell—I sprang to my feet, terrified. The sound often meant that a hand had slipped a letter under the door. I opened the letter, firmly resolving not to open the next one; yet I opened that too. What I read was irksome to me, tedious and as though dulled by excessive use, in spite of the words that stood out in capitals, underlined by a slashing flourish: "I am so made that, with me, SPITE is the active counterpart of gratitude." "Come, come my dear Colette." "Your farcical diplomacy in refusing to return that manuscript." "We have been partners, don't let us become enemies. I assure you that you would gain nothing by it. Our agreement, which is still in operation and on which I am still reckoning . . ."

But none of the letters ever asked me to retrace the steps that had taken me with my trunk and my dog and my cat and a little furniture from the Rue de Courcelles to the Rue de Villejust. And so, in the small ground-floor flat, I grew accustomed to the thought that here the flavour of my life must change, as the flavour of a wine changes according to the slope on which the vine is planted.

I know now that I was right to trust in what I then knew least, my fellow-beings, human kindness. If ever I set down my memories of the 'other slope' I feel that, by contrast, a groan of effort, a cry of pain, will have a joyful sound and that if ever I lament it will be happily.